challenge to the cities

An Approach to a Theory
of Urban Leadership

challenge to the
cities An Approach
to a Theory of Urban Leadership

HENRY W. MAIER, Mayor, City of Milwaukee

RANDOM HOUSE   New York

First Printing

© Copyright, 1966, by RANDOM HOUSE, INC.

Typography by R. Scudellari

All rights reserved under International and Pan-American Copyright
Conventions. Published in New York by Random House, Inc. and
simultaneously in Toronto, Canada, by Random House of Canada Limited
Library of Congress Catalog Card Number: 66-19852
Manufactured in the United States of America
by American Book–Stratford Press, Inc.

ACKNOWLEDGMENTS: Some of the comments in this book may be considered candid, but it should be kept in mind that they reflect one point of view. Others may well see some of the events covered here from a different viewpoint. Necessarily, because of the need to select cases to illustrate my points, I have not been able to give sufficient space to an adequate portrayal of the day-to-day achievements of the Milwaukee Common Council, which has given Milwaukee one of the best municipal governments in the country, or to the strenuous efforts of Milwaukee's civic leaders, its labor movement, its educational institutions, and its communications media —all of which undertake continuing civic responsibilities as a way of life.

I have worked on this book at odd hours, off and on, during the past five years, utilizing whatever spare time was available. Various people have helped with their suggestions. I particularly want to thank Dr. Henry J. Schmandt, Chairman of the Department of Urban Affairs at the University of Wisconsin-Milwaukee for his helpful comments. Others who offered valuable advice were Patrick Healy, Executive Director of the National League of Cities; Dean Stephen K. Bailey of the Maxwell Graduate School of Citizenship and Public Affairs at Syracuse University; and William L. Rafsky, executive vice-president of the Old Philadelphia Development Corporation.

H.W.M.

to MARY ANN, and to all other wives who share
the problems of public men

foreword

More than in most inquiries into human behavior, cliches cripple the understanding of politics. Economics now partakes of some of the magic of mathematics; psychology often probes private and fearful realms of life. But politics, especially in a democracy and especially at the level of local government, is "everybody's business."

From childhood on we are fed on simplistic folklore about how government should work and superficial new accounts of how it seems to work. From both sources, an overwhelming tendency to oversimplification appears. "Power tends to corrupt" we are told—where systematic examination of the sources of wrongdoing suggests the opposite. "You can't beat city hall" is still a national axiom, at least a generation after bosses and machines had disappeared from almost every city hall.

Most debilitating of all is the conviction that theory and practice in politics don't mix. Thomas Jefferson, John Adams, and Woodrow Wilson to the contrary, the notion persists that political scholars rationalize ideal worlds and political practitioners grapple instinctively, clumsily, and intuitively with reality.

It is Henry Maier's important—and happy—contribution in this account of urban politics to lay to rest this particular cliche. A professional and successful mayor of a large, complex American city, he is a practitioner who applies systematic knowledge about politics to the daily management of public affairs. How and why he does so—with success—is the subject of the readable and intriguing chapters that follow.

Other politicians have given us readable and intriguing memoirs, with sugar-coated reminiscence of campaign escapades and program crusades. Mayor Maier adds the component of theoretical rigor. He is concerned with developing and applying a theory of public leadership in an urban setting, and he achieves considerable success in this effort. D-STEPP is the shorthand for his basic formulation. Case studies, a clear grasp of the major thrust of modern decision-making analysis, and a working knowledge of small group theory comprise his techniques of observation.

The result is good reading and good theory. The case accounts of major decisions are set in a framework of Mayor Maier's attempts at strategy-making on central issues of urban development; his search for effective tactics; and his efforts to mobilize support—"enrollment" is his term. Thereafter, chapters on power and philosophy provide his explanations of why he proceeded as he did.

One learns, then, with surprise and pleasure (from an academic point of view) that at least one city in the United States arrives at its major decisions through a systematic, documented process of analysis, established as official form

M-25 of the Mayor's Office, a prescribed formal guide to decision-making. One learns that the Mayor's approach to the city council derives from six principles of small group relations. One finds that Budget Messages are defined, prepared, and published as tactical devices to compensate for mayoralty power deficiencies in other areas. With these innovations, municipal government can come to rival Secretary McNamara's Pentagon as a practitioner of new schools of management.

The theory Mayor Maier advances is by no means complete, but rather, in his words, an effort "to begin a beginning." Academicians may find some fault with the abstract underpinnings. Fellow practitioners may suspect some post-crisis rationalizations are involved. But the signal contribution is that the Mayor has made theory operational—and in the public interest. And that is what good research, reflection, and action are all about.

Finally, from the perspective of the Federal Government, itself deeply engaged in efforts supporting the emergence of more liveable and more human cities, books of this quality are welcome. They clarify the programs in which national assistance and aid are most useful. They encourage the development of a national urban policy initiated in the last two Special Messages on the Cities by President Johnson. And they help assure us that the critical ingredient to all our efforts—strong, intelligent, persuasive leadership at the local level—is forthcoming.

ROBERT C. WOOD
*Undersecretary of Housing
and Urban Development*

contents

challenge to the cities

An Approach to a Theory
of Urban Leadership

prologue

Morning

Consciousness dawns slowly and the Mayor's thoughts return to the night before. It had been one of those late, late evenings that never seem to end. After the meeting he had attended, he had allowed himself to be trapped in a lengthy and inconclusive discussion of a controversial city issue. He takes heart, however, at the thought that a visit with a certain alderman earlier in the evening had seemed quite productive. Despite their occasional differences of opinion, he really likes the fellow. He is happy that last night they re-established a rapport which had seemed to be fading.

While getting dressed, the Mayor thinks of another member of the city's Common Council. He thinks, "He's the kind of guy who remains silent unless he can say something bad."

He settles down at the breakfast table where his wife has served his usual, if somewhat unorthodox, breakfast menu:

one cookie, a glass of skimmed milk, and the first of at least a dozen cups of coffee he will drink during the day.

He picks up the morning newspaper and quickly scans the pages. He spots a particular item, a trouble spot, and reaches for the telephone. His working day has begun.

To the outsider, the Mayor's routine may appear simple: breakfast, telephoning, office, lunch, office again, dinner, evening speech or meeting, home. As Joe Citizen sees him passing by with a smile and a wave (part of a mayor's uniform), he may even be misled into thinking that the Mayor has an agenda unruffled by tumult, unfettered by frustrations, and never demanding of critical decisions.

Fortunately, Joe Citizen cannot hear this first phone call. "He's at it again," the Mayor says into the mouthpiece, and his voice is by no means a quiet purr. "Find out what the hell he's talking about this time." He gives further directions to the person at the other end of the line, hangs up, and begins to mull the matter over with his breakfast, though he continues to read the newspaper.

He remembers one of the times when the papers were hitting him pretty hard and he decided to quit reading them. He "kicked the habit" for a couple of days, but then curiosity got the better of him. Like most men in public life, he has found that continued activity is the best antidote for criticism; but so far he has never found an antidote for the pain in his wife's face as she reads an unfriendly news story.

Now his daughter is bustling around as she prepares for school. This sixth-grader couldn't care less about his morning reveries. Her daddy now becomes an answering machine for a whole battery of questions on a variety of

subjects. He finds her endless interrogations, interspersed
with an occasional flash of her wit, fascinating.

His wife tells him that the doorbell was rung again last
night late in the evening. He tells her that it was just kids.
"Some kids," she says.

She is heavily involved in the civic life of the city. In her
early forties, she looks astonishingly young and, as local
journalists have noted, is beautiful. In addition to supervising the home, she carries on an extensive local corre-
spondence, and attends many civic functions on her own as
well as most of the functions that the Mayor attends. At
such functions she often sits listening intently as a sound-
ing board for some of the ideas the Mayor may or may not
launch publicly in the near future. She likes her comple-
mentary role as the wife of a public official. What's more,
she likes and respects "politicians."

As the Mayor leaves the house, she gives him a memorandum of things she would like brought to the attention
of his personal secretary. For the most part, this pertains to
such matters as "thank you" notes she feels the Mayor
should send.

This morning as he rides to city hall, his thoughts are not
on the condition of the city streets, or the movement of
traffic, or the drabness of certain parts of the city, or its
beautiful new renewal areas. Although his image of the city
is like a series of map overlays—one for industry, another
for parks, others for housing, schools, landmarks—his mind
this morning is on the manscape with which he knows he
will have to deal during the day, rather than on the cityscape.

How is he to motivate the people he must move or

whose consent he must gain? How will he deal with his political enemies? How can he approach Mr. X, who doesn't seem to want to produce within the guidelines of a system mutually agreed upon?

Perhaps there is always lightning in the sky for a mayor, and the old city hall is always the potential storm center. But the cheerful doorman who greets him in the morning seems little aware of this as the Mayor heads past him, up one flight of stairs and into his office.

"Good morning," he says to the dark-haired little receptionist, who always reminds him of the female lead in *Flower Drum Song.*

"Good morning," she says brightly.

Soon after he arrives, his personal secretary enters his office. She is a former business secretary who joined him in his first campaign for mayor, and has stayed with him. She is efficient, loyal, and dedicated. She presents him with the early morning papers that he must sign and a picture he has been asked to autograph.

She calls to his attention an especially complimentary letter from a civic group. When there are unpleasantries in the news, she tries to counterbalance them with a special bit of good news. He grins privately at this tactful bit of consideration on her part.

He looks over his list of incoming calls left over from late in the previous afternoon, and asks about the call from the building inspector. The inspector wants to see him as soon as possible. The Mayor says that he'll see him immediately.

His city has a long-standing reputation for good housekeeping, but the Mayor had noticed upon taking office that the line policies seemed to be softening, and he means to toughen them up. The new inspector has been hammering hard at a number of violators in the central area. Of late, there have been rumbles of political retaliation.

When the inspector arrives it is this situation he discusses. The Mayor commends the inspector for his tough-mindedness. He knows the man is fair and he is unconcerned about the rumors.

The inspector has left, and the Mayor spends the next hour reviewing some reports on his desk. These concern his operational plans, the priorities for action that he has established, and involve a number of decisions. He tells his secretary that he wants to see the planning coordinator and the economic development director in the late afternoon.

Coming through the door with a big Irish grin on his face is a secretary who will be in and out of the Mayor's office several times during the day. He is the combination press secretary, troubleshooter, appointments secretary, political secretary, and operational subchief of staff—a man who truly relishes the challenges of the Mayor's office.

The secretary mentions a number of people whom the Mayor ought to see. They encompass every variety of personality: the labor leader who supports and the one who opposes; the businessman who gives and the one who takes; the citizen who smiles and the one who scowls; the big public spender and the "no public spending" variety.

The secretary informs him that the evening paper is doing a story on organized labor's influence in local government and wants to interview him on his labor appointees.

He informs the Mayor that a reporter wants to know if he will answer the governor's apparent criticism of the city.

He says that up until now the communications media

have not shown much interest in the Mayor's charter message, but it is still early.

He recommends acceptance of several civic invitations.

The Mayor discusses all items with him, accepts or rejects his suggestions, then with a grin tells him to get busy and turn out some work.

Later, taking a breather, the Mayor walks around the outer offices. He exchanges pleasantries with the quick-fingered stenographers. He strolls into the office of the assistant director of economic development. He likes to take a small break with this fellow because they have the same hobbies: fly fishing and hunting. The Mayor always keeps a small vise mounted somewhere at home and in his spare moments he painstakingly develops his latest fly, which he is sure will be a world-beater. The assistant director listens to his expectations with a tolerant smile. He winds up discussing some of the latest endeavors of the division of economic development and then returns to his office.

At noon he enjoys a luncheon with some members of the Common Council. He seeks out their reactions to various proposals and, where differences exist, tries to find a common ground.

Most municipal chief executives of the country seem to find themselves in open or covert conflict with the legislative branch of the government. Such conflict often exists simply because the legislative body zealously guards its prerogatives. Then, too, while the executive bears great loneliness and responsibility, the legislator often bears great frustration without adequate credit for a job well done.

The Mayor knows that at times the Council will ruthlessly defeat him on a project, perhaps embarrass him if it can (sometimes as a result of goading by would-be candidates for mayor), just to demonstrate its power. Usually, however, such an impasse occurs only if the Council has been repeatedly irritated, or if frustrations have mounted to the point where the members need a scapegoat.

When this does happen, the Mayor is professional enough not to condemn the Council to the point of severing relations and entering permanent combat, although some mayors may feel that combat is more worthy than programming and may choose it as a political way of life.

The Mayor finds, in attempting to advance his programs, that the number one cry raised against him in the Common Council is that he is seeking to expand his powers. He does not treat this too seriously because he knows that legislators use this attack only when it suits their purposes. And he knows that they know that one of his main functions is to present them with proposals of a major nature which they in turn can oppose or support as they wish.

He likes them and respects them. And within reasonable bounds he seeks their good will. In his city, with its form and traditions of government which permit practically no patronage, good will and patience are two of his best assets when it comes to promoting his programs.

Afternoon

Back in his office after lunch, the Mayor answers some of the telephone calls that have piled up since late morning. He meets briefly with the civil defense director. While a television camera looks on, he takes part in the ceremonial signing of a proclamation in his office.

After a while he leans back in his chair to relax for a moment, but his secretary flashes him on the intercom. "There is a gentleman here who insists on seeing you," she says, and gives him a name.

"Send him in," he answers. The door opens and a citizen walks in. He wishes to talk about a problem of much concern to him and his neighbors.

"A number of people in our neighborhood want to meet with you to discuss trucking on our street," the citizen says.

"All right, we'll hold the meeting," the Mayor says, "but all of the reports from our departments indicate that nothing can be done until the expressways are completed." He schedules the meeting, even though the local alderman has already informed the Mayor of the problem, regretfully remarking that there is no way to satisfy the citizenry immediately.

To his office now come his chief aide, the director of economic development, and the planning coordinator. Their discussion concerns all the Mayor's immediate dreams for the city, here in the form of 26 top-priority projects listed on the cards that lie before him on a table. The list includes matters as forward-looking as a long-range fiscal plan for the city, as prosaic as a proposed new system for combining the collection of garbage and refuse, as colorful as a potential world festival.

No matter what else occurs in his life as mayor, this list is never far from his thinking, for he feels that the city's future rests in turning these plans into reality. Most of his administrative resources are mobilized to accomplish the goals listed on these cards.

He knows that each program or project will take time— time for others to accept the idea, time to work out necessary compromises, time to get the matter in operation. Some of his projects will take longer than others, because they will require the consent of three other branches of government. Timing is the overriding consideration, and the small task force gathered in his office is dealing with that consideration in relation to each project.

When the meeting is over, the Mayor turns to the material he is preparing for a major policy speech. He calls two staff members for projections of estimated revenue needs for the next ten years. "We have some figures," one says. The Mayor asks questions about the basis for the projection and concludes that it is sufficiently sound. Then as an afterthought he says, "I don't suppose that anyone will pay too much attention anyway."

They smile. They know what he means. Having operated with him through both crisis and calm, they know the difficulties of communication.

Exit staff men. Enter the reporters assigned to the city hall beat. The Mayor's press relations are informal; only on a very important occasion does he call a formal press conference. By and large, he feels he has enjoyed a good relationship with the communications media in his city.

Most of the key editorial positions are filled with progressive people, although a few still tend to treat city hall as the greatest free show in the world.

Since there is no immediate "hard" news, the city hall

reporters are discussing the heat engendered by a recent appointment. "As you know, I thought you were going to be whipped on the confirmation," says one. "To tell the truth, I had my doubts, too," says the Mayor, without any self-satisfaction. He still regrets that a good man was forced to run the gauntlet to win confirmation.

The conversation ranges over a number of items on his program. The men currently covering city hall are bright young journalists. Maybe there are times when they press his office hard, but that's just part of the game.

Reporters are fond of writing about public figures they have known. The Mayor thinks that some day he would like to write about reporters he has known—about how some of them can read upside down; about how one dishonest devil would knock out part of a quote if it did not fit his preconceived theme of a story. There was one who wrote so many stories about the city's purchase of a new car for the Mayor that when the fellow came into his office and asked "what's new," the Mayor told him there was a citizen in a remote section of town who had not heard about the new car whom the reporter should go out and inform personally. There was another who could turn an intended facetious remark into a conflict story. When the Mayor protested, he met the worn defense used against public figures: "You're just supersensitive."

When the reporters leave his office, he continues to think about a variety of things touched on during their visit. Where can he gather the support to put across his state tax distribution program? How can urban renewal be speeded up? Delays resulting from the paperwork necessary between the local and federal governments seem to be causing much concern in areas slated for demolition. He wonders at what points he can compromise on his reorganization plan without giving too much away.

His mind flashes back to the meeting on priorities. Perhaps he has overcommitted his administration; on the other hand, there are so many city needs to be met. If only so much time didn't have to be consumed in trouble-shooting, he could get on with the development programs so much more effectively.

However, there's no getting away from it; it's part of the job. Ever present in local government is the spark of conflict. Many causes may bring it to life—causes ranging from poverty to frustrated civic pride, from the discontent of people living in a deteriorating neighborhood to the public outrage of baseball fans suddenly deprived of their major league team.

Evening

The typewriters are covered in the outer office and most people have gone home for the day. The Mayor is once again discussing a number of problems with his chief aide. He promptly decides some questions which require an immediate answer. They agree that several areas need further exploration before a decision can be made, and assignments are made for those who are to gather the facts.

Later, an old personal friend and wise political advisor drifts in, and the remaining time turns into a congenial discussion of politics. "How are we doing?" he asks his astute friend, and the friend with the sensitive antenna for public reaction gives him a rundown.

Finally, his security officer reminds him that he has a dinner engagement soon. As he reaches for his coat to head out into the night at the end of his office day, he may be thinking, "What was really done?" He had pleased the people who had received the proclamation and posed for a picture. Perhaps the luncheon with the aldermen had not come off as well as might have been expected, since they bogged down on a controversial issue. The world festival proposal was laid over again by a council committee. There were more criticisms of the city's development director, and the Mayor's sympathies are with the director. A new rumor had floated in that there is political trouble in some areas of the city.

At the convivial evening banquet, the Mayor is applauded by the audience. Afterwards, of course, there are those who stop him to lecture or advise. "Why don't you . . . ? "Why haven't you . . . ?" He thinks of the many different calls upon him for leadership, and he recalls how a friend, a former secretary to another mayor, had put it: "The great game is to destroy the mayor's authority, prestige, and status, and then call upon him for leadership."

He has his own definition of leadership. He must rise above the passions, the complexities, the perplexities of his daily existence to a conception of procedure that involves a total strategy of development for his community. He must be willing to run the gauntlet of indifference, misunderstanding of motive, and downright hostility to move his community in a forward direction. He might get re-elected by riding events and by capitalizing on dramatic conflict, but he will not amount to a tinker's damn as an institutional leader unless he is willing to take spade to the undramatic ground of development.

At home, his wife asks, "How did it go today?" "Oh, so so," he answers.

He makes a few telephone checks on various items, and then he finally relaxes. His day is over.

one *Background and Backdrop*

A new mayor takes office thinking that the moon over city hall is made of cream cheese and that all is peace and harmony on the cityscape. He has won his victory at the polls. He has received a heart-warming number of congratulatory telegrams, letters, and phone calls. His hand has been mauled by the cordial handshakes of old friends—some of whom he never knew before election day. It is still a bit strange to hear himself addressed as "Your Honor," but it sounds good. There is no question but that now all will close ranks and march shoulder to shoulder into that golden land of promise and progress.

By the end of his first term, the illusions are gone. Officially, he is still "honorable," but some are calling him by other titles under their breath. He may find himself blistered at times by the newspapers and subjected to barrages of attack from political opponents, opportunists, and the poorly informed. He has been taught that laudations are often little more than vocalized anticipations of benefits to come. His dreams have been scorched by experience.

Yet the experience has not been without value. His understanding of people, both as individuals and in the mass, has been deepened. His sense of realism has been sharpened during this baptismal period. He is more conscious of the need for a methodical approach to institutional leadership.

This book is about my own endeavors to achieve such an approach during my first term of office.

The Background City

When I took office in April, 1960, 36 other men, beginning with the city's founding father, Solomon Juneau, had preceded me as mayor of Milwaukee. At first, they had been drawn largely from the ranks of the Milwaukee pioneers, many of them Yankees from the East. Even Edward O'Neill, the Irish mayor who first won election in 1863, came to Milwaukee by way of Vermont. One of the last of the pioneer mayors was a lumber baron, Harrison Ludington, elected in 1871. By 1884, Milwaukee's growing German community was able to put one of its own in office, Berlin-born Emil Wallber.

Among my predecessors there had been the "happy mayor," George W. Peck (author of *Peck's Bad Boy*), who said in his 1890 acceptance speech, "There is nothing more pleasant in the world than to have people happy,"[1] and who resigned a few months later to become governor of Wisconsin. There was the "popocrat," David S. Rose, the mayor who promised all things to all people and whose wide-open policies gave Milwaukee a roaring reputation in the late 1890s and early 1900s. Another colorful figure was the "boy mayor," twenty-nine-year-old Sherburn Becker, who liked to officiate at local fires and is well remembered for his ax-wielding war against the sidewalk clocks used as advertisements for shopkeepers along Milwaukee's main street in the early part of this century.

The passing of one era and the beginning of another was no doubt symbolized by the election in 1910 of Emil Seidel, Milwaukee's first Socialist mayor, whose secretary was the poet Carl Sandburg. In Ludington's day, in the 1870s, such a phrase would have been anathema, but by 1910 Seidel could, in his inaugural address, praise the workers of the city as "its most valuable asset."[2] With the election of Seidel, Milwaukee municipal government entered a new phase, one that became well developed under the twenty-four-year administration of Mayor Daniel H. Hoan, another Socialist.

Hoan considered himself the manager of the "public business," which he insisted could "be conducted vastly more intelligently and efficiently than private business."[3] His accent was on municipal service, in the belief that "those communities are best which serve most." While scrupulously watching the public treasury for any signs of leakage or pilferage, Hoan placed municipal service before promises of lower taxes, considering it "not only poor sense but poor politics for a city official to be a moral coward." He should, he said, "cease apologizing for tax bills levied for meritorious needs and honestly expended funds; . . . he should go out and tell the people the truth and by so doing win the confidence if not the warm support of many of those politically opposed to him."[4] During Hoan's tenure as mayor, Milwaukee's reputation for city services was unmatched among cities of its size.

"To the outside world," one commentator notes, "Hoan, the Socialist, was the symbol of early twentieth-century Milwaukee; and his reputation for honest, vigorous, and democratic municipal administration, as well as his outspoken championship of his working-man constituency— qualities which kept him in office rather in spite of than because of his connection with Socialism—identified the veteran mayor, more than any other person, with the forward strides of the Wisconsin city in its adjustment to the problems of the maturing metropolitan scene."[5] It should be noted that, while Hoan himself wore the Socialist label, his Common Council did not.

In 1940, Hoan finally went down to defeat before a handsome, popular thirty-two-year-old nonpartisan named Carl Ziedler. In 1942, young Ziedler enlisted in the merchant marine and was lost at sea. Aldermanic president John L. Bohn succeeded him as acting mayor, and in 1944 was elected to a full term. He was succeeded by Carl Ziedler's brother, Frank, a Socialist, who in 1960 chose not to run after a twelve-year administration.

When Mayor Solomon Juneau addressed the first Milwaukee Common Council in 1847, he marveled that there was now a city of 7 square miles and 12,000 inhabitants where, eleven years earlier, the "soil was unbroken."[6] At the beginning of Mayor Hoan's administration, Milwaukee's population was climbing toward the 400,000 mark; when it ended, twenty-four years later, in 1940, the population of the city was 587,000.

In 1960, when I took office, Milwaukee was the eleventh largest city in the nation, with a population of 741,324, in an official metropolitan area, since enlarged, of 1,194,290. Unlike that of many other central cities, the population of Milwaukee is still growing, owing largely to annexation and in-migration, and our Community Renewal Program projects a population of 1 million in the 96-square-mile central city area by 1985.

As in many other cities, growth has been accompanied by pains, and the question in 1960 was whether these were the pains preceding a rebirth of vitality, or the creaks and groans of an old age that would degenerate into decrepitude. The situation had not changed materially since newspaperman Richard Davis wrote, a decade earlier, in *Our Fair City*, "Milwaukee is not engaged in building a great city. Here and there are signs of a quiet ferment working. But the town is resistant to change."[7] How to overcome this resistance was one of the challenges that faced me the day I took office.

While Milwaukee is justly noted as the nation's brewer of beer, it can more appropriately be called the machine shop of the Midwest. Since the opening of the St. Lawrence Seaway, the waters of Lake Michigan have connected its port directly with the ports of Europe and the Orient, contributing to its international trade. It is in large measure a workingman's city, with manufacturing employing about 40 per cent of the work force, and the county ranks as the nation's ninth largest industrial producer. It is also a city where home ownership ranks high on the value scale; about 48 per cent of the families in the city own their own residences. In 1960, the overall unemployment rate was 25 per cent higher for all Standard Metropolitan Statistical Areas (SMSA) than it was for the Milwaukee SMSA. While the median family income for the Milwaukee area was nearly 11 per cent higher than that of all other SMSA's, every level of income below $6000 was more common inside the city than outside the city. The median family income in the City of Milwaukee was $6664.

There's still much truth in the popular picture of Milwaukee as a city of Old World charm and the easy-going good nature, good living, and geniality typified by the German word *Gemutlichkeit*, since there is a higher proportion of population with German antecedents here than in other areas. The German imprint can still be seen in many of the city's institutions and in some of its older architecture, but the city is no longer the "Deutsch Athen" of America, a name it once wore with distinction. In the early years, nearly two thirds of Milwaukee's population was foreign-born, including large numbers of Irish and Germans. By the late 1890s, however, the city's American-born inhabitants outnumbered the foreign-born by the same margin of two to one. The city's share of foreign-born had dropped from 64 per cent in 1860 to 7.7 per cent in 1960.

"Milwaukee's cosmopolitan flavor is primarily second-generation," reports our Department of City Development. "Actually, a smaller proportion of Milwaukeeans are foreign born than in the typical SMSA. A considerably larger proportion than average are children of foreign-born parents—more than one person in five in Milwaukee, as compared to one out of six for all SMSA's."[8] Although Milwaukee is about four times as German as the average urban area, it is also twice as Polish as the average, as measured by 1960 census data on foreign-born and second-generation population. In addition, at least thirteen other major ethnic groups are represented, and all contribute their distinctive flavor to the city's mix.

Recent years have also witnessed an increase in the Negro population. In 1960, the 62,458 nonwhites made up 8.7 per cent of the population of the central city. In 1965, the city department of vital statistics estimates the nonwhite population at 80,641—10.2 per cent of the total. (In 1950, nonwhites composed just 3.6 per cent of the city's population.) It is significant that only 2 per cent of the Negroes in the Milwaukee metropolitan area live outside the central city, the lowest percentage of Negroes outside the central city in any of the SMSA's with a population of over 1 million.[9]

Politically, the city has long been characterized by independence and freedom in municipal politics. Since 1912, local elections have been on a nonpartisan basis, and there are times when the Common Council represents the nineteen different points of view of the individual aldermen and the mayor a twentieth. Public issues are threshed out in an atmosphere of freedom that has changed only in degree since cannons were fired and a minor civil war nearly erupted in a dispute about the location of a bridge across the Milwaukee River in 1845. There is widespread citizen representation on the various boards and commissions of the city, and if a private citizen doesn't get a hearing on a particular issue, it is not for lack of opportunity. The people, moreover, expect the mayor to lend his ear to neighborhood opinion, and a great amount of his time is taken up with ceremonial appearances.

Like many other central cities, Milwaukee is hard put to find the resources to meet the growing service demands of a central city. The Citizens' Governmental Research Bureau of Milwaukee estimates that in 1964, $1,086,000,000 was collected in taxes from all sources in Milwaukee County. Of this sum, two thirds, or $689 million, went to the federal government. The state collected $219 million, and the county collected $178 million.[10] A portion of the state's take is returned to the municipalities in the form of state aids and shared taxes. In 1964, approximately 24 per cent of the city's revenue came from this source; however, as the city often laments, the system of aids and taxes is so out of balance that suburban municipalities may receive up to 100 per cent of their revenues from this source and, on the average, do receive at least 53 per cent of their revnues. This imbalance is one of my twenty-six prime targets—a revised distribution setup for state aids and shared taxes to relieve the heavy property-tax burden borne by the Milwaukee taxpayer.

Government within the metropolitan area is greatly fragmented, and at last count, there were 46 taxing units within Milwaukee County. Other than the City of Milwaukee, these include 18 suburban municipalities, each proudly waving its own flag of independence emblazoned, "Don't invade me." There are also 22 suburban school districts, 2 sewerage commissions, 2 city school boards, and the county government itself.

Further evidence of fragmentation is found in the tax bill

paid by Milwaukee city residents, which includes taxes to the Milwaukee Board of Education, the Milwaukee Board of Vocational and Adult Education, the Milwaukee Sewerage Commission, and Milwaukee County. Despite the fact that the city's share is about one third of the total, taxpayers all too often merely look at the total at the bottom of the bill and launch missiles of malediction in the direction of highly visible city hall.

The Milwaukee County government, with a budget in the same range as that of the city itself, is well developed and undertakes a number of functions. Almost half of the county budget provides for welfare assistance and county-wide health and hospital facilities. The county government also maintains 10,000 acres of parks, directs expressway construction, supervises the county stadium, airport, zoo, and conservatory, and provides a system of courts.

Since 1960, the county has been headed by an elected county executive with power to prepare an executive budget, to coordinate administrative and management functions, and to make appointments with the approval of the county board of supervisors. He also holds veto power over the actions of the 24-member board. Seventy-two per cent of Milwaukee county's 1,036,041 residents live within the central city, and 18 of the county supervisors are elected from districts fully within Milwaukee's city limits. But this has not necessarily meant that programs favored by the city have been automatically accepted by the county government.

Perhaps because of unfortunate experiences in the lands of their forefathers, democratic Milwaukeeans have, over the years, kept a careful check on the reins of government.

While we still operate under an 1874 city charter which, until 1965, specified detailed procedures for the Commissioner of Public Works to follow when purchasing horses or horse feed for the fire and police departments, major revisions in that charter have succeeded in placing checks on the powers of the mayor. As a result of scandals, in 1911 the legislature removed the police and fire departments from the mayor's direct supervision, making both chiefs heads of their departments with responsibility for the enforcement of the law vested in them. "Though the clause that makes the mayor chief executive was not directly repealed," Mayor Hoan noted, "his powers were modified and no direct means are now provided by which the mayor can enforce his orders against either department."[11] The accompanying chart shows how people, mayor, and council choose members of city government in 1965.

A good evaluation of mayor-council relationships appears in a report of the League of Women Voters of Milwaukee, which states:

> The mayor of Milwaukee is generally regarded as having a weak position in relation to the council, since he cannot prepare an executive budget, makes few important appointments without council approval, cannot legally terminate the service of an unsatisfactory appointee before his fixed term expires, and has no direct administrative authority over department heads. On the other hand, he does have the power to veto which can be overridden by a two-thirds vote of the council.

However, as the League pointed out, and as we shall see in Chapter Two in the section entitled "Tactics of the Executive Budget Message," the lack of an executive budget is not necessarily a handicap. As the League puts it:

THE CITIZENS OF MILWAUKEE ELECT:

THE MAYOR   THE COMMON COUNCIL
(elects City Clerk)

CITY ATTORNEY	CITY COMPTROLLER	CITY TREASURER
4 yrs.	4 yrs.	4 yrs.

SCHOOL BOARD
15 members, 6 yrs.
(elects
Vocational Board
5 members, 4 yrs.)

THE MAYOR APPOINTS
WITH COMMON COUNCIL APPROVAL

FIRE & POLICE COMMISSION 5 members 5 yrs.	DEPARTMENT OF CITY DEVELOPMENT Director 2 Years coordinating the work of Plan Commission Housing Authority Redevelopment Authority	SEWERAGE COMMISSION 5 members 5 yrs.
DEPARTMENT OF BUILDING INSPECTION Building Inspector 4 yrs.		DEPARTMENT OF PUBLIC WORKS Commissioner 2 yrs. Engineer 3 yrs.

HARBOR COMMISSION 5 members 3 yrs.	PARKING COMMISSION 7 members 3 yrs.	SAFETY COMMISSION 18 members 3 yrs.	BOARD OF REVIEW 5 members 5 yrs.
BOARD OF APPEALS 5 members 3 yrs.	HEALTH DEPARTMENT Health Commissioner 4 yrs.	TAX DEPARTMENT Tax Commissioner 3 yrs.	BOARD OF ASSESSMENT 5 members 5 yrs.

THE MAYOR APPOINTS

CITY SERVICE COMMISSION 5 members 5 yrs.	LIBRARY BOARD 9 members 4 yrs.	MUSEUM BOARD 9 members 4 yrs.	ELECTION COMMISSION 3 members 4 yrs.

VARIOUSLY CHOSEN

BOARD OF ESTIMATES 11 members ex-officio	AUDITORIUM-ARENA BOARD 11 members 6 City representatives ex-officio	BOARD OF PURCHASES 7 members ex-officio

MEMBERS OF VARIOUS PENSION BOARDS

NOTE: This chart is adapted from the City of Milwaukee's "1965 Directory and Report of City Progress in 1964."

The mayor's presence on the Board of Estimates and its budget examining committee gives him an opportunity to work out budget matters with the staff and with those aldermen on the finance committee. Here he is able to include those program items in which he is most interested and once the budget is worked out and presented to the council, it is unlikely that it will repudiate its own finance committee by voting it down. The mayor has an item veto in budget matters, also. In fact, the give and take between the mayor and a small number of aldermen may result in a final budget more to the mayor's liking than an executive budget worked over by the finance committee on its own.

The study noted that "the council might be described as weak in some areas also, because of a lack of overlapping terms, demands from each alderman's home ward, the number of boards and commissions which are delegated to carry on important parts of city business, and the difficulty of a single alderman to gather an outstanding portion of the spotlight shared by the council as a whole." "Despite these weaknesses in structure," the study concluded, "Milwaukee government has a proud history, is nationally regarded as one of the finest municipal governments, its accomplishments have frequently pioneered in new fields of municipal responsibility, and its departments are often cited as being outstandingly honest, efficient, and purposeful."[12]

The citizens of Milwaukee are also noted for their integrity, and people say this is a fine community in which to bring up children. Many people within the city view the city as a service organization, one that takes care of streets, sewers, snow removal, refuse disposal, and the like. Many see it as a home. They enjoy its variety of attractions, whereas others who have fled to the picture-window utopias of suburbia look upon it as a place of drabness and noise—a fine place to earn their incomes, but they wouldn't want to live there.

Viewed from the mayor's office, Milwaukee is a galaxy of people of different ethnic origins and of organizations—churches, labor unions, businesses, schools, welfare societies, manufacturing companies, and others. It is a living organism whose strength is in its diversity. To keep it strong and healthy requires, above all, mastery of all the tools of the new municipal sciences and employment of institutional leadership, for, as it grows older and as it changes, new diseases threaten the body politic and new remedies must be applied as soon as the symptoms make their appearance.

The Gap in Research

In recent years there has been a great deal of research on the urban community. In a sense, sections of the "lost world of municipal government" have been discovered. Universities are beginning to establish departments of urban affairs, and research grants for urban study are mounting. There is expanded activity in the professional associations of municipalities. The Congress is awakening to the recognition that most of our people now live in urban complexes and that the proportion is mounting steadily—as steadily as urban problems and the pressures on traditional modes of local leadership.

A key figure in the new world of urbanism is the mayor or chief executive of the large city. He occupies the only position that can provide overall leadership to cope with the demands of the modern urban polity. But his position is not a simple one. He faces multiple pressures and problems as complex as our society. His life is complicated by the fact that he must be one part institutional leader, one part political leader, one part educator, one part scapegoat, and some other part for whatever purpose his community wishes to use him. Of his various roles, however, that of institutional leader stands out as basic and crucial.

A mayor consequently needs a way of thinking—a theory or philosophy—about his office, as do others in assessing the office. One of the first endeavors (amid the pressure of events) that a new chief executive might profitably undertake is the development of a strategy of leadership. As he searches for the tactics to implement it, he will also begin to develop a philosophy or system of leadership.

Current literature will be of little help to him in developing a model of public leadership. In fact, a comprehensive review of research in the field points out that the published literature on the "nature of public leadership" constitutes a major research gap.[13] My comments are an attempt to help fill this gap. They represent a way of thinking about the role of the municipal chief executive, a local public leader with omnibus responsibilities of leadership.

In my mind, and in the minds of the many other mayors and public officials from across the country with whom I have talked during the past few years, closing this gap should be one of the most serious concerns of urban research. For the nature of leadership is deeply involved with the question: How do we proceed to solve our urban problems? We certainly cannot continue to proceed as we do now to send a man out to hunt bear with a slingshot.

We have to find out how this man can better equip himself and what armaments others can provide him.

Floyd Hunter's methods and premises in his pioneer study of community power[14] have now been largely discredited. His attempt to get the ball rolling, however, can never be discredited. So, too, my methods and premises may be discredited and greater wisdom employed in some similar effort, but this is my attempt to "begin a beginning." In this attempt, I have necessarily drawn from my own experiences and presented cases as they developed around my own seat of office. The case studies used here have a unique function: they have been selected and written to give the reader a feeling of occupancy of a role of public leadership, the role of the mayor of a central city. In effect, I invite you to look over my shoulder.

They do not have the purpose, as does the usual case study, of illuminating all the circumstances that are relevant to a decision and of exploring all the causes that had direct influence on the outcome. They are limited to one man's perspective.

NOTES

1. Bayard Still, *Milwaukee* (Madison: The State Historical Society of Wisconsin, 1948), p. 296.

2. *Ibid.*, p. 279.

3. Daniel W. Hoan, *City Government* (New York: Harcourt, Brace and Company, 1936), p. 183.

4. *Ibid.*, p. 101.

5. Still, *op. cit.*, p. 531.

6. *Ibid.*, p. 109.

7. Richard S. Davis, "Milwaukee: Old Lady Thrift," in Robert S. Allen (ed.), *Our Fair City* (New York: The Vanguard Press, 1947), p. 191.

8. Department of City Development, *Milwaukee's Population Trends, Characteristics and Projections* (Milwaukee: Department of City Development, 1963), p. 45.

9. Advisory Commission on Intergovernmental Relations, *Metropolitan Social and Economic Disparities: Implications for Intergovernmental Relations in Central Cities and Suburbs* (Washington, D.C.: U.S. Government Printing Office, 1965), p. 236.

10. Citizens' Governmental Research Bureau (Milwaukee), *Bulletin* No. 9, Vol. 52, Dec. 22, 1964.

11. Hoan, *op. cit.*, p. 198.

12. The League of Women Voters of Milwaukee, *City Government— Part II, A Study of the Structure and Operation of Milwaukee City Government with Particular Emphasis on the Mayor-Council Relationship*, 1965, pp. 7–8.

13. Wendell Bell, Richard J. Hill, and Charles R. Wright, *Public Leadership* (San Francisco: Chandler Publishing Co., 1961), pp. 182–83. See also Charles Press, *Main Street Politics* (East Lansing, Mich.: Institute for Community Development, 1962).

14. Floyd Hunter, *Community Power Structure* (Chapel Hill, N.C.: University of North Carolina Press, 1953).

two The D-STEPP Formula

For many years the classical POSDCORB formula was regarded as the accepted way of looking at the institutional responsibilities of the office of chief executive or administrator.[1] The formula, Planning—Organizing—Staffing—Directing—Communicating—Reporting—Budgeting, still constitutes a good description of the main tasks of the public executive. It labels the kinds of activities he carries out and the problem areas he encounters. But it fails to account adequately for and describe the mayor's actual involvement, the requirements of his institutional leadership, and the procedural concerns of his operation. These facets of the mayor's role can better be described by another formula, here referred to as the D-STEPP formula, which is more compatible with contemporary administrative theory: Decision making—Strategy—Tactics—Enrollment—Power—Philosophy. Succeeding chapters will discuss each of these facets and will illustrate them with cases drawn from my own experience.

The term *institutional leadership*, as used here, means

responsible leadership that attempts to make the municipal machinery run more efficiently, to prevent disorder in the use of resources. It also refers to the effort to improve the character and the resources of the institution involved.

So the "D" in the formula represents the *decisions* that the chief municipal executive must make to preserve order, to gain efficiency in the operation of the municipal plant: often such decision is of an "either-or," "yes-or-no" type. Sometimes a problem of major proportions that originates from outside is propelled into his considerations by the actions and commitments of others, and its proportion and very presence of necessity give it top priority on a mayor's agenda. As we shall see in the Brown Deer and 72nd St. Library cases, he cannot escape responsibility in this area if he is to exercise even a minimum of institutional leadership. There will also be suggested a formal method for handling the making of decisions.

The "STEPP" of the formula represents the ingredients of creative leadership, the making of choices. Expressed in the most simple terms:

1. *Strategy* is the mayor's total planning perspective, the overall design of his objectives.

2. *Tactics* is his procedures to implement the strategy.

3. *Enrollment* is both his specific and his broad efforts to enlist people in support of his objectives.

4. *Power* is his capability to effect results.

5. *Philosophy* is his system of leadership as exercised through his understanding of the demands of institutional leadership and the ways of people.

The D-STEPP formula is the framework for the proposal implicit in this study: a model for operational procedures for the municipal executive, a possible way for the analyst and the scholar to test local leadership, and a guideline for understanding the mayor's problems for those who would help him to help them as members of the local community.

In this analysis, developmental strategy and tactics are interwoven in the three chapters that follow because they are inseparable in execution. Both the Department of City Development and the Community Renewal Program, for instance, are involved in the city's long-range development goals, but the immediate problem of bringing them into being was one of the step-by-step procedures. Enrollment and power are also treated together because, while separable they are often closely intertwined. The analysis proceeds to show how one mayor's office uses a formal method of dealing with certain types of decision-making problems.

But beneath the surface of this presentation are implicit questions that require further study. For example: How can a mayor control his agenda as he strives to exercise policy leadership? What ought to be expected of this man as an institutional leader amid the "foul-up factors" that so often obstruct his approach to basic community problems? These and numerous questions like them are related to the unique nature of public leadership—an animal far different from private executive leadership if for no other reason than the great visibility of the public leader.

Although the cases presented here are particularized illustrations, they demonstrate the institutional problems that a mayor is likely to encounter. Again it must be kept in mind that the attempt here is to develop a potential model of the role of top public leadership. Every situation has different variables, and each of the cases discussed here falls into a different category of leadership problem. Each, however, is similar in that it involves decision-making, relationship of strategy and tactics, or problems of enrollment and power; each tends to illustrate a different basic aspect of the considerations of leadership.

The cases are not intended to portray substantive matters. The case on the initiation of the Social Development Commission, for example, is not intended to portray either uniqueness of approach or the stage of development of Milwaukee's efforts in this area. It, like the others, is intended to illustrate the particular situation and outlook of a mayor in the process of exercising public leadership.

NOTE

1. Luther Gulick, "Notes on the Theory of Organization," in Luther Gulick and L. Urwick (eds.), *Papers on the Science of Administration* (New York: Columbia University Institute of Public Administration, 1937), p. 13.

three S for Strategy, T for Tactics

In today's complex urban society, in which fundamental choices must be made between alternative uses of resources, the old processes of choice no longer suffice. Perhaps there was a time when not too much harm was done if the public leader made his choices by intuition, by yielding to pressures, or by parceling portions of the candy-stick to as many as put out their hands for a share. Today, this method of procedure is as likely to be effective as would trying to fly a supersonic jet cross-country without the aid of an instrument panel.

It is true that a city government has many sources from which prospective choices can originate. Worthwhile proposals can come from a line department such as Health, from an overhead department such as Budget, from various members of the Common Council, from civic organizations, from the communications media, and sometimes from a citizen's letter. The center for the choices that lead to broad programming, however, must reside in the mayor's office. It is in this area of choice—of mapping a strategy of leadership and devising the tactics to implement it—that the mayor determines whether or not he is really a creative public leader or simply a problem-solver or a fire-fighter.

Although strategy is important in mapping the long-range course to his goals, the mayor cannot be concerned with it alone. Plans are only paper until they have been carried out, and a mayor's concern is the city of reality, as well as the city of dreams. He must employ tactics and make continuous efforts to see that plans are executed. Too often, I think, the concept of mayoral leadership is that of a man dramatically enunciating the "oughts" of city life without consideration of the day-by-day effort necessary to execute the steps that must be taken toward concrete achievement. That type of leadership can be as ineffective in its own way as the kind of caretaker leadership that tries to patch up the problems of today, leaving tomorrow to take care of itself—when, indeed, today's problem is often merely yesterday's problem postponed.

But I do not intend to imply that the mayor can take on the entire task alone. He must seek new and improved centers for the initiation of choice in attacks upon urban problem areas and in attempts to build the good city. Departments of Public Works, for example, were set up to initiate choice in the matters of sewers, streets, traffic control, and the like as their complexity called for technical knowledge and attention to detail beyond the range of the municipal policymaker. To meet the new problems of growth and change that beset the modern city, the mayor needs new municipal institutions to deal primarily with broad programs that go beyond the simple housekeeping chores of yesteryear. Setting up such centers of choice must be a central consideration in carrying out a strategy of leadership.

Strategically, too, the mayor must remember that city problems and the various facets of city development are interrelated and that the city must develop on many fronts at once. Economic problems are tied in with social problems and problems of physical development. The need is for the development of a cooperative circle in which progress in one sector helps progress in the others; ways must be found to break the vicious circle of a declining tax base which leads to a lack of fiscal resources to meet the need for development of wasted human resources which contributes to increasing areas of blight.

Resources are always a root problem. The mayor is in the best position to see that they are deployed according to the greatest need and for the best advantage in the long run. He may have to take steps to implement his city's resources and work for a better share of state and federal resources for his city.

From the day he takes office, the mayor must ask himself such questions as:

What should be the priorities for the economic, social, and physical development of the city?

What can be done to institutionalize action in those problem areas and developmental areas where there is as yet no accepted center for rational decision making or the initiation of rational choices?

How can a base for more integrated community action be established?

As we shall see, no system can eliminate entirely the "foul-up" factors, the personal feuds and ambitions that help create the mayor's hidden agenda. No system can eliminate conflict, but it can provide a better basis for resolving it. Nor can any system eliminate entirely the pleadings of special interests, but it can confront them with reasoned priorities and a surer public policy based on sound thinking and research in depth that wins a broader public backing.

Thus, one of the mayor's tasks of institutional leadership is to see that he has developmental centers from which recommendations can flow around a rational plan of priorities matched with resources. If necessary, he must take on the job of organizing, because without such institutionalized approaches there can be no effective planning. Such centers must be at the core of his strategy of leadership.

The cases that follow discuss some attempts to institutionalize efforts to meet some of the modern problems of my city. They grew out of a strategy of development which recognized the interrelated aspects of our city's problems. They grew out of the answer to the question: What organization can best coordinate the many individual and group efforts, gather the facts, set the goals and priorities through analysis, and supply the creative inventiveness that is necessary as a basis for future decisions?[1]

The answer will be affected, of course, by the nature of the problem—whether it is physical, economic, or social. But, in approaching any organizational innovation, one must always keep in mind that it is a step-by-step process in a free society.[2] An innovation, like any other choice, to be accepted must not stimulate too great a fear of change. There are exceptions, but in the main, revolutionary proposals simply cause explosions without results—often a disappointing revelation to the impatient presbyopic. Before presenting the cases themselves, a brief discussion of some of the innovations for which I have worked might better illustrate this point.

One of the cases discussed in the following chapter is that of the Department of City Development, the first major administrative reorganization in Milwaukee's city government in decades. To the casual observer, it appeared to be carried out in record time, but much negotiation and the working out of a consensus among many groups were necessary before it was finally an accomplished fact. When the idea for the department was presented to the Common Council, it did not involve an all-encompassing reorganization calling for abolishment and re-creation of all existing institutional arrangements for planning and redevelopment. It was presented as the most advanced acceptable step that could safely be taken without stimulating so much opposition that the proposal would be delayed interminably or killed. It laid the groundwork, however, for the next step: a survey recommending further reorganization.

As the organizational arrangements evolve, so should the program that represents the formal processes of public decision making. This is illustrated by cases dealing with the establishment of the Milwaukee Department of City Development and the creation of the Social Development Commission (see Chapter Four). As the cases indicate, these agencies must work out approaches that enable them to set priorities in terms of developing the community's total resources, human and material. Both demonstrate the importance of planning for a program of action—action based upon calculated decisions, upon alternative use of resources, and upon the practicalities of development within the limits of available resources.

Another organizational innovation, the Division of Economic Development (see Chapter Five), is attached directly to my office. Its scope and goals require that it look beyond its own immediate resources and toward the community at large for resources to forward its program. To succeed, the division must look to the universities and to civic and labor groups for the kind of research referred to as "an economic base analysis" that will (1) show the strengths and weaknesses of the local economy, (2) reveal the interrelationships of basic industries so that future programs can be aimed at those which have a potential in our city, (3) provide a basis for a realistic decision for city capital investment designed to strengthen our economic base, and (4) give general insight into the direction in which the local economy is likely to go.[3]

These programs or approaches are interrelated. Areas laid down by the Community Renewal Program, for example, can be used by the Social Development Commission to construct social profiles including such data as unemployment rates, spending habits, public assistance statistics, crime incidence, and similar information.[4] The Community Renewal Program, moreover, can provide the bridge between programs of physical and social development. Intimately related here is the program of economic development that can grow out of the activities of the Division of Economic Development and the concomitant basic research. What then begins to emerge is a pattern of total development with closely integrated features.

Still another decision must be made after the previous

operations—economic, social, and physical—are fully planned and programmed. This pertains to a long-term financial plan. There must be injected into the decision-making processes an increasing awareness of the effects of the state and federal governments upon the financial resources of the local polity. Local resources are today seriously affected by the manner in which higher levels of government levy and distribute taxes.

The organizations and programs referred to—physical, economic, social, and financial—will involve the total community: public bodies, private agencies, universities, social agencies, all citizens. Achieving this broad involvement and coordinating this overall approach to the needs and problems of the community is a time-consuming and demanding task. A strategy of this nature is likely to be criticized at first for moving slowly, but a chief executive must be willing to pay this price if he wishes to exercise sound institutional leadership.

NOTES

1. Harvey S. Perloff, *Planning and the Urban Community* (Pittsburgh: University of Pittsburgh Press, 1961), p. 106.

2. C. E. Lindblom, "The Science of Muddling Through," *Public Administration Review*, vol. 19, no. 2, Spring 1959, p. 79.

3. Charles M. Tiebout, *The Community Economic Base Study* (New York: Committee for Economic Development, 1962).

4. American Society of Planning Officials, *The Community Renewal Program: The First Years*, A Report prepared by Jerome L. Kaufman, Principal Planner, American Society of Planning Officials (Chicago: American Society of Planning Officials, 1963), p. 12.

four S for Strategy, T for Tactics:
Community-wide Programs

Forming the Social Development Commission

As is true of so many problems facing the chief administrators of America's large cities, Milwaukee's "social problems" were produced primarily by disruptive change which
rendered obsolete, at least in part, the administrative machinery geared to transact the business of the city. Perhaps
because the waves of migration of nonwhites and rural
whites hit Milwaukee relatively late in comparison with
other cities, perhaps because sizable portions of our people
cherished strong ethnic ties and traditions militating
against the spread of such problems as the growth of large
numbers of the unwanted old or the rise of systematic and
self-perpetuating juvenile delinquency almost approximat-
ing gang warfare, Milwaukee for years regarded herself
somewhat complacently as more fortunate than her sister
cities.

As the uncomfortable consciousness grew that perhaps it
could happen here, just as it had happened in Chicago and

New York—that perhaps Milwaukee *did* have a few problems which could stand looking into—interested and community-conscious citizens began to demand that city government do something to alleviate existing problems and prevent their recurrence. These groups for the most part insisted on confining the problem to a particular racial group or to a particular geographic area.

Provoked by an incident in the involved area, the Mayor's Study Committee on Social Problems in the Inner Core Area of the City was formed in 1959. The study concerned itself with 5.63 square miles, or roughly 7 per cent of Milwaukee's total area (the percentage is now much smaller because of the city's growth in area in the interim).

Within this area lived virtually all Milwaukee's non-white population. Always focusing (at least by inference) on the preponderance of Negroes within the area, the study took into account such factors as health, culture patterns, public welfare caseload, problem families and individuals, education, acculturation and manpower needs, schools, churches, leisure-time facilities, organization for social service needs, facilities for youth, the housing problem, and law enforcement (covering such areas as adult arrests, juvenile delinquency, and police-community relations).

The studies were exhaustive and produced a minute listing of the problems of this fragment of a city held up to a magnifying glass.

Unfortunately, recommendations for alleviating the problem were few, and in at least three instances the study committee made note of and deplored the fact that no single agency existed with the authority to deal with the full range of problems found in the "inner core."

When I took office in April of 1960, the "Inner Core Report" had been recently completed.

It sat monolithically on my desk, an incontrovertible (and almost indigestible) mass of facts, figures, statistics, and bleak reports of conditions as they existed, comprising a funereal picture of the lives and prospects of Milwaukee's rapidly growing nonwhite minority.

Almost immediately, powerful voices in the community began to demand that "Mayor Maier do something about the Inner Core," that I "implement" the Inner Core Report. Many of the "criers" had never read the report.

The people making up the Inner Core Study Committee consisted of some of the most able and enlightened members of Milwaukee's citizenry. They turned out a report which thoroughly examined the nature of the problem in the study area, made some intelligent surmises as to why specific problems developed, and made a few recommendations for coping with these specifics.

The recommendations were, necessarily, not sharply in focus. Some of the items listed were: motivate Negroes to learn skills to give them greater job potential and meet the city's needs for skilled labor; motivate Negroes to avail themselves of the existing "adequate" educational opportunities.

It would not have been feasible to make more specific recommendations—who should provide this motivation and how to go about it—because no agency existed with jurisdiction over multifunctional social problems.

The lack of such an agency was a key facet of the problem confronting me in April of 1960. Another was the fact that impatient citizens persisted in demanding that the mayor do something about the "inner core," disregarding the fact—and it loomed large to me as I wrestled with the problem—that social problems existed elsewhere in our community and could not be neatly confined within the geographic limits of a particular section solely because the characteristics of the Negro minority living there happened to dovetail with the popular definition of "social problem." It seemed to me that any unilateral action by the city could not stand a chance of reaching satisfactory, lasting solutions because the city simply lacked the power to exercise certain functions integral to the success of any attack on social problems.

I rejected in my own mind any fragmented, less-than-wholehearted attack on social ills, because such an approach would be inconsistent with my strategy for total community development. In view of these facts, a tactical plan evolved over the first months of my administration—a plan for coping with Milwaukee's social ills and for providing a framework for a coherent pattern of human development.

The case that follows will not attempt to delineate fully all the ramifications of the substantive issue of social problems. Instead, it will outline the series of factors and crises which arose in Milwaukee on this explosive issue of human rights and development.

My goal, stated simply, was this: to build a mechanism for cutting across boundaries of ethnic or class areas, across municipal boundaries, and across arbitrary divisions of jurisdiction and responsibility by creating an agency charged specifically with dealing with social problems. This agency was to operate wherever in the metropolitan area problems might exist by marshaling all available community resources and coordinating a multitude of agencies in a concerted attack on social blight.

The struggle to implement this plan presented me with a complex problem in institutional leadership. Unlike the situation for many of the other programs, success here was absolutely dependent on organizing a number of autonomous agencies, both governmental and private, none of which owed the slightest fealty to the office of Mayor of Milwaukee. Complicating the procedure were the demands of those who wanted immediate action in the inner core alone and the subterranean mutterings of what appeared to be a sizable number opposed to any city program attacking social problems and, particularly, to any expenditure of tax revenues in the Negro area of Milwaukee.

The first attempt to get a coherent, community-wide social development program involved an application in September, 1960, for a Ford Foundation grant to finance the initial effort. The application asked for approximately $750,000. Foundation trustees turned the application down, stating that Milwaukee did not qualify under the Foundation's criteria for this sort of grant. The application was amended, reworked, and resubmitted. Foundation executives then showed some interest in Milwaukee's problems and its potentialities for such a program. They visited the city, paying particular attention to the relationships between city government and the county, school superintendent and school board, and similar agencies.

Milwaukee again lost out. The Ford Foundation announced a $2 million grant to Oakland, California—which, in 1957, had organized "Associated Agencies," originally set up to control disruptive youth in an all-out community effort to alleviate some of the racial tensions produced by a series of gang conflicts between mobs of racially antagonistic teenagers.

The lesson was not lost. The Ford Foundation at that time was not interested in financing a city program against social problems, but would support a cooperative, community-wide program to deal with these vital issues.

[Note: In January of 1963, the director of public affairs for the Ford Foundation was reported as saying that the grant was denied because of lack of leadership in Milwaukee, where the mayor, according to a newspaper quote, was afraid of being called a "nigger-lover." The newspaper later amended its report, saying that the director had really stated that the mayor in any city with a project to help Negroes would have to stand up to the charge of "nigger-lover." At the time these remarks were made, an agency to work for the social betterment of all underprivileged residents of the Milwaukee area, and intended to "help Negroes" as part of its function, was in the process of formation. Several of the participating bodies had already indicated approval, but one of the key agencies—the county government—still hung in the balance. And these inflammatory statements, coupled with the prominence with which they were displayed in the newspaper, created a very real fear in my mind that reluctant members of the County Board might use them as an excuse to justify county abstinence from the program.]

After Milwaukee's rejection by the Foundation, I began working to pave the way for the creation of the sort of agency that would be attractive to foundation trustees. I also directed efforts toward expanding the sort of city services likely to be needed in a major social program and toward integrating other functions of city government into a limited social-problem approach. At the same time, I began conferring with representatives of institutions directly concerned with social development.

When general consensus was reached with these individuals on the need for an organization to coordinate the work of agencies handling problems in underdeveloped areas, in May of 1962 I initiated proceedings designed to effect this objective. First, at a meeting of about 50 people representing government, schools, and civic social agencies, I outlined my views on the need for a coordinating agency. Next, I issued a call for suggestions as to the composition and functions of such a body and charged the Milwaukee Commission on Community Relations, an arm of city government dealing directly with human rights, with the task of collating the suggestions and making recommendations outlining the form and jurisdiction of the coordinating agency.

By mid-June of 1962, the Commission on Community Relations had assimilated suggestions made by a wide variety of agencies and formally submitted its recommendations for organization to me. The proposed structure set up a number of committees consisting of organizations working primarily within broad functional categories, such as education, recreation, employment, churches, and police and correction. These functional committees would elect

chairmen who would make up an implementation committee. The latter in turn would make recommendations to a
policy committee, which would be charged with setting
priorities for action in various social problem areas and
supervising the lower bodies in putting the priorities into
effect.

At the top of the whole pyramid stood the mayor, who
was responsible for appointing the policy committee.

The plan had certain advantages—for example, it
brought all agencies concerned with the same problem
together in an organized structure for concerted action
within particular problem areas—but it failed to meet the
objectives of my basic tactic.

It made the mayor of Milwaukee responsible for appointing the policymaking board for what was ostensibly a
county-wide organization—yet it gave the Mayor's Office
absolutely no authority in the board's decision making. It
made no mention of funds and implied that budgetary
requirements would be supplied by the city alone, creating
the automatic and valid criticism that the city had no
business paying for a program benefiting the entire county.
Perhaps most important, the plan did not ensure full
representation and participation from those agencies—both
governmental and private—which I believed must support
a coordinating commission if its actions were to carry any
weight in the community.

Another major objection to the organizational structure
developed by the Community Relations Commission was
the proposal to utilize the commission's staff to provide
services for the new agency. In my judgment, this would
necessarily have had the effect of making the new organiza-

tion a mere adjunct of the Community Relations Commission and of limiting its horizons to problems of a racial nature.

These drawbacks compelled me to what the entire carefully planned system of meetings built around the impartial Community Relations Commission had been designed to avoid—the drafting of a plan for the new agency by the Mayor's Office rather than by the relevant participants, thus making the task of enrolling the latter more difficult.

Nevertheless, I submitted a plan to the Common Council on July 28, 1962. It called simply for the creation of a coordinating body with equal representation from the five agencies directly concerned with social problems in the Milwaukee metropolitan area—city, county, school board, vocational school, and United Community Services, which represents a multitude of voluntary agencies.

It was decided to call the new agency the Community Social Development Commission (later the name was changed to the Social Development Commission of Greater Milwaukee), to make clear from the outset that this body was not to be merely a race relations group or a study or discussion group or an "inner core" agency. Instead, I wanted to accent the idea that its establishment would mark the foundation of a new concept for the Milwaukee community—a joining of hands, a marshaling of forces to bring to bear all available resources in an attack on urban social ailments wherever in the community they might exist, whether their victims were young or old, black or white.

Beginning with the Common Council message of July 28, 1962, I began my campaign to enlist the five agencies—

city and county governments, Milwaukee School Board, vocational school, and United Community Services—as participants in the new commission. The message stated several basic themes which were to be emphasized throughout the fight for the creation of the Social Development Commission:

1. That social problems sprawled beyond geographical boundaries and were too complex for any one agency, working on its own, to handle adequately
2. That modern techniques developed for planning the physical renewal of our cities were capable of being adapted to plan the human renewal of underprivileged city dwellers and to set priorities of action in dealing with social ills
3. That the resources already existed for a comprehensive attack on social problems but that new resources would have to be developed for new programs, and that eventually the federal government would enter this area
4. That an active partnership must be set up, all of the agencies bearing some responsibility for social developmental programs to knit these diverse and unrelated programs into a cohesive whole

Tactically, however, these basic themes received varying degrees of emphasis, and additional factors were brought into play as, in the next six months, I made personal pleas before all the proposed participants in an effort to enroll them in this new program.

To the Common Council, for example, I pointed out that the city's powers were limited principally to physical, health, and protective services which, while essential, did not reach the causes of the conditions they sought to remedy. I pointedly suggested that festering social problems engendered a geometric increase in the amount of police and fire protection and health services the city must

provide and that problem areas consumed a disproportion-
ately high share of the city money provided for those
services. I noted that, while the limitations of city government made an effective unilateral city program against
social problems impossible, the fact that the larger problem
areas were located within the city limits led to the "natural
expectation" that the city government would assume the
primary role in seeking and bringing about solutions.

Because some aldermen were concerned with the Inner
Core Report, I stated that any coordinated effort would
have particular effect in the critical core area of the city. I
also pointed out that precedents existed for cooperating
with other units of government, such as the committee for
coordinating the work of the city, school board, and county
park commission in the field of recreation. Finally, I presented the aldermen with the opportunity to become
leaders in this virtually unprecedented new program and to
take the initiative in securing the consent of the other
agencies to weld separate programs into a single program of
meaningful cooperation.

At the committee hearing on my recommended resolution, I again appeared before the aldermen to explain the
program further and to attempt to clear up doubts that had
arisen between July 28, when I submitted the resolution,
and September 24, 1962, the date of the hearing. I pointed
out that this was not the mayor's plan, but a synthesis of
the thinking of community leaders in various capacities,
including many of the aldermen. I emphasized the orienta-
tion toward action of the proposed program, to meet the
criticism voiced privately by some of the aldermen that the
mayor was "grandstanding" on human rights and was creat-

ing a "talk agency" to smokescreen the problems of the Inner Core Report.

Since the council had relatively recently approved unanimously a comprehensive Community Renewal Program, I attempted to carry their sentiments to this new field, calling the suggested community-wide effort a "community renewal program of human development to remedy sociological sores and prevent their cancerous spread." And I pointed out that, while an increasing number of voices were telling city government what *should* be done in dealing with sociological problems, little had been heard on *how* it could be done. I stated flatly that studies such as the Inner Core Report could do little to provide solutions simply because no official body existed to implement their recommendations and assign priorities of action.

While the resolution was pending before the Common Council, I did not neglect the effort to develop widespread community support for the new agency. I held repeated private conferences with representatives of the other agencies and community leaders in business and labor and with influential newspaper and television executives. And in public appearances, I continued to hammer home the basic themes of the commission and to call for enthusiastic public understanding and support for the agency.

The Common Council on September 28 unanimously approved the creation of a Social Development Commission and urged the other agencies to join in. The resolution went through with only one amendment—instead of immediately authorizing funds, the council decided to make money available as needed from the council's contingent fund. Armed with the council's backing, I then began a series of appearances, virtually hat in hand, before the other proposed constituent bodies requesting their participation.

The School Board's Committee on Appointment and Instruction approved the commission on the same date I appeared before them, and its recommendation was instrumental in surmounting opposition to the commission when the full school board met a week later. At that time, one of the school directors moved that the board delay approval until the city established its own clearcut policy on such issues as inner core housing, equal housing opportunity, open space in the core area, and action possibilities for the new agency.

He asserted that the commission would be "just another excuse to delay solving pressing community problems" and warned that the commission might "stall at coming to grips with the problems." Pointing out that the commission was expected to be a working agency and that its effectiveness could not be known until it was tried, the School Board defeated the move for delay and approved the commission.

The Vocational School Board and the United Community Services speedily indicated approval of the commission, and four of the five agencies were in.

The remaining agency, however—the county government—was perhaps the most important, since it alone was responsible for administering the county's giant welfare programs and such other necessary functions as the extensive county park system, with its varied recreational opportunities. And the County Board proved to be the most difficult of the agencies to enroll in the Social Development Commission.

I first appeared before the board's Committee on County

Institutions on December 3, 1962; my appeal was to the supervisors as government professionals, and I stressed the organizational need for a coordinating commission.

For elected officials everywhere, questions of taxes and expenditures are perhaps preeminent whenever any new program is being considered. Consequently, along with repetition of the basic themes of the commission, I stressed the financial implications of lack of unified action. I pointed out that a large share of the county's welfare budget was being spent in the underdeveloped areas of the community; that the welfare budget was constantly rising; and that additional expenditures were apparently not able to check the rising tide of juvenile delinquency and similar ills. I added that the commission would be expected to serve as the receiving body for foundation and/or potential federal funds (the federal government's War against Poverty had not yet begun) and that under the proposed structure no one participating agency could dominate the commission's actions or impinge on the authority of the individual agency in its own sphere of action.

Also appealing for county participation were representatives of the other agencies, which had already joined the city government in the commission plan and had, in fact, appointed some delegates to the commission's governing body. But after one supervisor told the committee that the proposal "looks like another attempt to get government money for a private function," the committee voted unanimously to refer the plan to the County Corporation Counsel for a legal opinion. That body's opinion, released on December 19, was an unexpected blow to the commission movement. It stated that Wisconsin law prohibited the county from contributing any funds to the commission since such an agency was not a specific public purpose within the list of purposes for which the county could levy a tax. The opinion also stated that the county could participate in the commission if it did not contribute funds. Chances for such participation, however, appeared dim.

The prohibition against county funds made the provision of a budget for the commission virtually impossible, since it could not realistically be expected that Milwaukee's Common Council would magnanimously provide enough money to pay the city's share of operation and the county's as well. After almost a year's work, with victory virtually in hand, it seemed that the commission would never effectively materialize or that its creation would be delayed until the carefully nurtured crest of public enthusiasm had subsided into unconcern and apathy.

On January 15, 1963, the County Board's Institutions Committee gave token approval to the commission by instructing the preparation of state legislation authorizing financial contributions when and if the County Board decided to participate. I was now forced to make the best of an unsatisfactory solution. To preserve what had already been won, I sent a plea to the County Board to authorize limited participation in the commission without financial obligation. I added—though this was not what I would have hoped for the commission—that funds would not be necessary for the Social Development Commission until representatives had been appointed and given a chance to meet and until a course of action and staff and budget requirements were agreed on.

I followed the message with a meeting with the chairman and two vice-chairmen of the County Board. Finally, on March 13, it was agreed that a resolution would be introduced before the board calling for limited county participation. I again had to pledge, before winning agreement, that the commission's status would be "purely advisory" and that it could not determine policy for any of the governing bodies. On March 20, the board approved the resolution, and the major stumbling blocks to the Social Development Commission were finally surmounted.

Meanwhile, I had directed vigorous city support and guidance for the legislative bill authorizing county financial contributions. After several versions of the bill had been drafted and passed in and out of committee several times— one version contained a spate of noble words but failed to include the authorization to contribute money—the legislature finally approved county financial support early in 1964.

But by this time the effectiveness—and possibly even the continued existence—of the commission had been threatened by new crises. Community leaders had evidenced widespread support and enthusiasm. Uniform editorial support for the new commission had been forthcoming—the late William Norris, chief editorial writer for the *Milwaukee Sentinel*, said, "The new commission will be of inestimable value" and foresaw "unlimited opportunities [for the commission] for study, guidance and collaboration with all agencies of government concerned with the socioeconomic problems of a great, expanding metropolis." Then an unfortunate, ill-chosen statement attributed to one of the new commissioners created widespread controversy and may have alienated one of the groups whose confidence the commission most desperately needed, Milwaukee's growing and increasingly aware Negro population.

At one of the first meetings of the ten commissioners—one appointed by the governing body and one by the executive branch of each of the five member agencies—the group indulged in what was apparently a general discussion of what the members thought the goals of the commission should be, what some of the problems were, and what could be done about them.

In this context, the commissioner appointed by the County Board Chairman allegedly made some remarks that had instant repercussions among the Negro community. Among other things, he was reported to have said that Milwaukee should consider methods of keeping the "ignorant poor" from moving to this community and, referring to the fact that his teenaged son had been severely beaten by two Negro youths who were never identified, that Negroes looked so much alike that it was impossible to tell them apart and that "many of them have an I.Q. of nothing."

By these ill-considered remarks, reported to have been made casually at a public meeting, the commissioner made of himself and the entire Social Development Commission an inflammatory *cause célèbre* in Milwaukee civil rights history and gave emerging rights groups an issue around which to organize and attract converts.

In a *Milwaukee Journal* story sampling Negro reactions to the statements, these quotes are found: "If [the commissioner] had said something like that about a Polack, Lord have mercy! City Hall would have been blown up by now." "If you're ignorant, as [he] says, they [white people] are the cause of it. They want to keep us ignorant."

Demonstrations were quickly organized to capitalize on these sentiments in the Negro community. First, members of a newly formed chapter of the Congress of Racial Equality (CORE) picketed the County Board Chairman's office in the courthouse, demanding the removal of the commissioner. Getting little satisfaction from the chairman, they then conducted a "sit-in" in his office and were arrested and charged with disorderly conduct. Next CORE demanded that I inform them whether I agreed or disagreed with the statements attributed to the commissioner and followed this demand with another, that I repudiate him and effect his removal from the commission.

In my answer, I stated that I did not agree with the stark statements quoted in the press, but pointed out that the statements might have been taken out of context and perhaps did not fully represent the commissioner's views.

CORE immediately expressed dissatisfaction with my answer. In response to a request for a meeting, I agreed to meet with their representatives privately, at breakfast, so that we could discuss the situation frankly without fear of further aggravating racial tensions. The meeting, however, proved fruitless. Meanwhile, CORE had started a sit-in campaign in my office to attempt to pressure me into removing the commissioner. Neither I nor anyone from my staff interfered with this campaign in any way, but demonstrators were ultimately arrested for disorderly conduct when they refused to leave City Hall at night to allow custodians to clean up.

In a public statement, I attempted to explain that I was without authority to remove the controversial commissioner. I said that CORE was demanding an approach which "legally I cannot take, and morally I would not take."

Milwaukee's liberal, enlightened labor movement condemned the statements attributed to the commissioner, but the author of the statements that started the controversy was not without some support within the community. This support became more vocal as reaction to CORE's demonstrations and sit-ins developed. Letter-writers defended both his right to express an opinion freely and what the writers considered the soundness of his position.

A group was organized to circulate petitions supporting the commissioner and the County Board Chairman who appointed him. The chairman, a Democrat, spoke before Republican organizations and intimated that the demonstrations might have Communist overtones. He claimed that his mail favored retaining the commissioner in a ratio of 90 to 1. A state senator from a predominantly Polish district proposed legislation prohibiting sit-ins. "It's no longer a peaceful demonstration when people lie around the floor like pigs," he declared.

James Farmer, CORE national director, claimed Milwaukee was one of the "most segregated cities in the country," and stated, "I can't think of any major city in the North where an appointee to such a commission, having made such statements, would have been retained." Farmer offered to debate the chairman and his commissioner, both of whom declined and, in passing, criticized the mayor on civil rights progress in Milwaukee.

The incident, relatively insignificant in itself, had developed into a springboard which both activists and conservatives were using in the civil rights controversy. The real function of the commission was being forgotten.

The *Milwaukee Journal*, in a front-page editorial, clarified the picture, calling the entire episode "overblown," and warning that misdirected energy being consumed in the controversy was detracting from the important business of the commission. The *Journal* added that CORE had made its point—a statement with which I heartily concurred—and injected a note of reason into the affair by pointing out the obvious fact that the stated goals of CORE and of the commission pointed in the same direction.

Meanwhile, the commission—the only body other than the appointing authority with any control over individual commissioners—submitted the entire issue to the city Commission on Community Relations. The latter eventually adopted a report stating, in effect, that the commissioner "sincerely regretted" his "unfortunate" statements and that, if retained on the commission, he could make constructive contributions in the area of social planning. The commissioner served out his one-year term without further incident and was succeeded by another appointee.

So the affair eventually died a natural death. But in its lifetime it created serious repercussions affecting the growth of the commission, took vital time and energy away from the commissioners in the crucial formative period, and introduced a divisive element into a concept whose very essence was partnership and cooperation.

The remarks of the commissioner—if he was quoted correctly—certainly did not represent the kind of thinking needed on the fledgling commission. But I, as mayor, was absolutely powerless to remove him from office or even to officially rebuke him since he was the official appointee of the Chairman of the County Board. Moreover, my intervention would have destroyed the carefully planned and painstakingly created concept of equal partnership among the member bodies, with no one agency empowered to exercise control over any other agency.

So I stood virtually mute, powerless to act even if I had chosen to, while the protests mounted, the sit-ins took place, and some support for the sentiments allegedly uttered by the commissioner spread through certain segments of our population.

And in the meantime, the dream of a unified attack on social problems of every variety seemed to go by the boards as the controversy received great emphasis in the news. In the process, the Social Development Commission of Greater Milwaukee began more and more to be considered by the public as strictly a civil rights agency created to work with Negroes in the "inner core." After well over a year of work and constant emphasis on the multifunctional goals of the commission, we had come full circle. Milwaukee was back to the Inner Core Report kind of thinking all my efforts had been designed to avoid.

This sort of thinking even returned to some members of the Common Council, who had unanimously and enthusiastically passed the initial resolution calling for a single agency to coordinate all social programs in the community. While the commission was still embroiled in the controversy and its aftermath, preventing full organization, setting of objectives, or determination of staff and budgetary needs, a resolution was introduced in the Common Council calling for the creation of a City Commission on the Aging. This commission was to work independently of any other agency (such as the Social Development Commission) to coordinate those programs for the elderly operated by or exclusively within the city. The creation of such a commission would have substantially cut into the jurisdiction of the Social Development Commission, probably resulted in less serious attention to its budget requests, and served as a precedent for further inroads into the SDC's functions with the creation of still more limited agencies.

In opposing the city commission, I had to fight the accumulated distorted concept of the SDC's function and goals and some newspaper coverage which rallied support behind the city commission. "Maier Against Commission on Aged," the first headline read. Buried well down in the story was the explanation that I felt we already had a commission for the aging in the Social Development Commission. Thus were alienated great numbers of the elderly —in an election year.

To try to remedy the situation, I requested the opportunity to address the Social Development Commission in order to make my views clear and to make some suggestions as to priorities.

I pointed out that, from its very inception, the SDC was designed to coordinate the work of the various agencies dealing with the problems of such segments of our population as the aged, the indigent, the young, and the unacculturated. To clearly assert its jurisdiction over these and other areas, I suggested, the commission should take affirmative action in some of these problem areas.

As an illustration, I discussed several facets of the problems of the aging and recommended that the commission set up an advisory committee with these tasks: analyzing and defining the problems facing the aging in Milwaukee, taking inventory of agencies already working in the field, and making recommendations for effecting a partnership between these agencies and such additional services as might be necessary for an integrated, coherent program for the elderly on a community-wide basis.

I told the commissioners unequivocally that this sort of action was absolutely necessary if Milwaukee was to take advantage of its unique opportunity to lead American cities in a pioneering concept. I stressed the need for immediate action to make the commission a vital, operating agency which could qualify for federal assistance in any program the federal government might institute to prevent social blight from strangling our cities.

The commission immediately took steps to begin operating on a program basis by appointing its own advisory committees for problems of the elderly and of the young.

Its action, however, did not forestall attempts to create a separate city commission. Powerful forces in the state capitol, it was rumored, were most concerned in this election year with mobilizing the elderly by reaching them with periodic newsletters designed to build a bloc vote. Their justification for the continued attempts was that the Social Development Commission was burdened with "monumental tasks" and that to allow it to function in the area of problems of the aging would heap additional burdens upon the commissioners and do a disservice to the entire community.

An organization called the Milwaukee County Nonpartisan Committee for the Aged lobbied with the aldermen for a city commission. And the president of the Milwaukee Metropolitan Area United Auto Retired Workers Council stated that my position would cost me the support of retired workers. "Any time a committee of people approaches the mayor and they represent 100,000 votes, it's good business for him to listen," he said.

The unfortunate thing about the whole affair was that a good many old people, many of whom probably desperately needed attention, supported a city commission that would have been made up exclusively of elderly persons. They were to be given no staff, no funds, and were to be purely advisory to the Council, with no authority to initiate action. Worse, they bitterly opposed the Social Development Commission's activity in this field, an opposition stirred up by broadside mailings claiming old people were being "relegated" to a mere subcommittee.

Proponents of the separate commission measure organized an intensive campaign of support, and once again I had to marshal my own supporters to speak to the aldermen and appear before the deliberating committee. Finally, I appeared before that committee myself, opposed the city commission, and offered a substitute which endorsed the Social Development Commission as the proper agency to work with problems of the elderly.

The committee eventually adopted my substitute, but then found the matter referred back to them by the Common Council. The supporters of the city commission were not giving up, and for some time the status of the measure was shrouded in mystery while attempts were made to line up a majority. The proponents of a city commission failed to muster sufficient votes, and the problems of the elderly remained with the Social Development Commission, which eventually survived both controversies and was fully organized as the federal War on Poverty began.

On December 16, 1964, President Johnson announced that a Community Action grant of $312,565 had been allocated to the Social Development Commission of Greater Milwaukee, one of the first grants to large cities under the Economic Opportunity Act of 1964. In January, 1965, the commission was instrumental in getting Milwaukee selected as one of the first eighteen locations in the nation for a Youth Opportunity Center with an additional five-year authorization for a $3,500,00 program for Milwaukee. The director of the Milwaukee district office of the Wisconsin State Employment Service said at that time that Milwaukee's center would be one of the first of the eighteen to actually begin operations because of the close relationship the Employment Service has had with the Social Development Commission and because of the progress the commission has made in developing a Community Action Program.

Projects involving all phases of the Economic Opportunity Act have been developed under the commission's aegis. By the end of 1965 more than $5 million in federal funds had been allocated for these projects which will help alleviate poverty and its attendant problems among the young, the aged, and the unacculturated, Negro and white, wherever they may live within the metropolitan community.

Most of this money will be spent where poverty is most

heavily concentrated—among the people who were so thoroughly and clinically examined in the Inner Core Report. The Social Development Commission is attempting to act as a catalyst, as an originating and coordinating body to develop new programs and focus old programs where they are most needed. Unquestionably, President Johnson's policies with regard to poverty, as expressed in the Economic Opportunity Act, gave the commission the money and the stature necessary to do the job. But it gives me great personal satisfaction to realize that Milwaukee was ready with an agency meeting immediate federal requirements even before the War on Poverty was announced.

But our readiness to begin the war was not a sign that all controversy was at an end. Ironically, some of those who said the commission would be dominated by politicians and would therefore be ineffective in the sensitive political area of human rights and human development now claim that the politicians exercise too little control. The commission can only make recommendations on matters within the jurisdictions of the governmental bodies represented on its board, but it can also act directly on its own or contract with private agencies for specific services or projects.

For example, in its role as Community Action Agency, the commission gave approval to a proposal for planned parenthood clinics to provide birth control information in poverty areas. The commission acted after lengthy study, discussion, and a six-hour public hearing at which proponents and opponents of the project were bitterly articulate and strongly partisan in expressing their viewpoints. Elected officials in both city and county government expressed their disapproval, and Milwaukee's Common

Council adopted a resolution urging that the project application be turned down. I ordered a report on the legal status of the commission and determined that it was legally empowered to act in this matter free of control from any member body. I therefore allowed the Common Council's resolution to go into effect without my signature as the aldermen's expression of opinion on a vital and controversial issue.

The commission chairman informed me privately that the commissioners were hesitant about going against the council's wishes, but approved the project anyway because they felt almost unanimously that over-large families among the chronically and hereditarily poor were a major contributing influence to the perpetuation of poverty. The commissioners therefore acted independently, exercising their best judgment and disregarding heavy pressures which were brought to bear on them and which have continued. While the approach they took is not necessarily one to which I subscribe as mayor, I have stated repeatedly to the many who now demand that I do something about "my" commission that there is nothing I can do. It is no longer— if it ever was—"my" commission. Instead, it is an independent agency in the process of mounting a total program against all aspects of poverty. It is free of political control and—because its members do not depend on elections to maintain their sensitive and unpaid posts—free of the fear of having necessary but unpopular decisions challenged successfully at the ballot box.

Here is a case where the mayor's chief role was that of an innovator. A problem existed whose solution required more than the forces of his own political jurisdiction. His work was to envision the kind of body needed to meet the need and to take the lead in bringing together the other units of government and agencies needed to constitute it. Now that the commission is formed, his formal authority consists simply of his power to appoint one of the commissioners. His city stands to benefit, however. Because there is such a commission—and because President Johnson has made poverty a vital national concern—Milwaukee stands a chance of finding some real solutions, instead of mere palliatives, to long-standing social problems.

I do not delude myself, however, that the commission or its actions are fully accepted. I expect that controversy will continue as long as the commission—in common with similar agencies in other major cities—keeps trying new approaches for solving social problems. But if controversy is the price of innovation, the cost of originality is cheap. It is manifest that the old techniques are no longer sufficient to cope with the human problems of our cities.

Establishing the Milwaukee Department of City Development

For more than seventy years Milwaukee has had official agencies designated for planning, beginning with the official Park Board set up in 1892. Over the years, this board had a succession of names, becoming in turn the Milwaukee Park and Planning Board, the City Plan Commission, the Board of Public Land Commissioners and, once again, the City Plan Commission.

In the past two decades, two new agencies have entered the planning picture. In 1944, the Housing Authority of the City of Milwaukee was created as a separate body corporate and politic. In 1958, the City of Milwaukee set up a Redevelopment Authority. Milwaukee has therefore never suffered from a lack of planning activity, but it became apparent in recent years that there were too many planning generals going to battle in all directions with little or no coordination. The trouble was the lack of administrative machinery for ensuring that a blueprint for city development was properly drawn and carried out.

Here was the situation I found when I took office in April of 1960:

The *City Plan Commission*, a city department with both staff and line functions, was in charge of the preparation of a master plan and was responsible for some aspects of administration of the zoning law.

The *Housing Authority of the City of Milwaukee*, a separate corporate body established by the state legislature, was charged with the construction and management of public housing for low-income or veterans' families. It was the city's agent for providing low-rent housing and incidental slum clearance, and as a matter of policy, the Common Council had determined that new public housing projects should be located in blighted areas.

The *Redevelopment Authority*, another corporate body authorized by the state legislature, was charged with the planning and carrying out of redevelopment projects and was designated as the local public agency for dealing with the federal government for such projects.

From the strictly functional standpoint, there was duplication of effort in many areas, such as land acquisition, property disposition, maintenance, and project planning.

Within a few months of taking office, I was firmly convinced that our urban renewal efforts suffered more from lack of overall direction than from anything else. When it came time for the city to draw up a Community Renewal Program, a dispute developed between the City Plan Commission and the Redevelopment Authority over the question of which agency should undertake the program. When the city planner was asked to work out a plan for lakefront development, he reported at the last minute, after a lag of several months, that a resolution by the Common Council was required before he could undertake the work. I was beginning to see the obvious truth of the statement in *The Exploding Metropolis* touching on the mayor's role in planning:

> Expert as professional planners may be, planning is ultimately a line rather than a staff function. To be effective, it requires the mayor's active support and coordination. It is here more than anywhere else that he is required to serve as a center of leadership and responsibility: if he is unwilling to mesh planning and execution, no one else can. In too many cities, the mayor has abdicated this responsibility, and when he has, planning becomes an exercise in futility.[1]

As the situation became more entangled, it seemed to me that the only answer was a single authority with one department head. In October, 1960, I made brief public mention of the idea at a meeting of the Citizens' Urban Renewal Committee, suggesting that city functions of urban renewal, public housing, city planning, and housing code enforcement probably should be in a single department. "In the back of my mind," I told the committee, "is the idea that eventually we would have one development agency in the city to take the place of several which now exist separately."

Late in 1960, the hearings on the 1961 municipal budget provided an occasion to focus the Common Council's concern on the whole problem of unification of city planning. At that time I insisted that additional planners be provided for the Plan Commission. A proposed increase in personnel can almost always be counted on to stimulate discussion among aldermen, and the members of the Finance Committee were soon discussing not only finance, but also planning. Why do we need additional planners? What are we doing with the planners we already have? What kind of planning is being done by the Plan Commission? Does this conflict with the planning by the other city departments and the Redevelopment Authority?

The council finally provided the additional planners, but in the process the important basic question had been successfully raised: Wouldn't our planning be more effective if there was one directing head to keep it on course?

In February, 1961, I held a discussion with an alderman who had more interest in urban renewal than some others because of the redevelopment projects undertaken in his ward. The Redevelopment Authority at this time was attempting to secure civil service tenure for its executive director, who was on leave from a teaching post at the University of Wisconsin at Milwaukee. The alderman opposed this move and was now favoring better coordination of planning activities. After our meeting, the alderman introduced a resolution in the Common Council requesting that its Organization and Methods Committee study methods of coordinating urban renewal programs and the advisability of creating a Department of Urban Renewal. He also requested that various personnel actions by the Redevelopment Authority be held in abeyance pending the report of the Organization and Methods Committee.

The committee met to consider the resolution through April and May. It compared the city's urban renewal organization with those in other cities. It made a study of the relationships of activities of the Building Inspection Department, the Health Department Division of Housing, the Citizens' Planning and Urban Renewal Committee, and the Planning Coordinator in the Mayor's Office.

My own thinking on the subject had been sharpened by outside reading. For instance, I knew that in Oakland, California, there had been a "reorganization of city departments, an increase in personnel, and a centralization of responsibility so that, administratively, urban renewal could proceed." New Haven had a centralized plan and was making excellent progress. I was convinced more than ever that this was the only way Milwaukee could move more quickly in the field of urban renewal and development.

In April, 1961, a state-wide referendum removed one of the big legal obstacles to effective urban renewal in Wisconsin. For some time I had been involved in the campaign to repeal the state constitutional requirement that a jury must rule on each parcel of land desired by the city to determine whether or not it was needed for public use. Now the people of the state voted to repeal the so-called "jury verdict of necessity provision," permitting the city to use its power of eminent domain more freely, without the danger of lay juries' carving up project areas by excluding parcels of land. The referendum victory would help speed up the entire urban renewal process, and this seemed to me added reason for creation of a central department to push development on a coordinated basis.

On May 3, I appeared before the city's Organization and Methods Committee, which, as its name implies, sits as a watchdog to eliminate waste and recommends procedures for developing greater efficiency in city government. I stressed the importance of quick action on the pending legislation. Because the state legislature was tied up with tax matters, there was no chance that legislation could be passed that year to consolidate the separate authorities established by statute. The alternative was for the council to set up a Department of City Development with a full-time director and for each of the agencies involved to appoint the director as its own secretary or executive director.

At this point two developments made the time opportune for me to move toward the goal of a separate department. The Executive Secretary of the City Plan Commission had retired, and the Executive Director of the Redevelopment Authority had given notice that he was leaving. Thus the executive positions for two of the three bodies that would be involved in any consolidation would soon be vacant, eliminating opposition that might develop from an executive appointee with a vested interest. If I pressed for action before the annual summer recess of the Common Council, there was a good chance that a department could be set up the same year. If no action was taken before the August recess, it would be too late for budget action in the fall for the new department. If the matter were held over for study, a number of roadblocks in the way of a unified urban renewal department might develop—not the least of which was the possibility of solidification of opposing attitudes over time. Accordingly, I pressed for action before the recess, pointing out that if there was to be a department in 1961, action would be needed soon so that departmental requests could be ready for a budget hearing in the fall.

In July, a proposed charter ordinance was introduced into the Common Council for the purpose of combining the functions of the three agencies. The ordinance was introduced by title only, because the final phases of the plan had not been agreed upon.

On July 18, I let it be known that I was in favor of a plan creating a Commissioner of Urban Development on the same administrative level as the Commissioner of Public Works and the Commissioner of Health. His department would combine the functions of the Redevelopment Authority, the Plan Commission, and the Housing Authority. I also indicated that I might favor the transfer of the housing division of the Health Department and the Building Inspector's Office to the new department, and possibly even transfer of the Division of Economic Development from my own office.

On the evening of July 20, 1961, I held an informal meeting of the council's Buildings-Grounds-Finance Committee in my office to go over the details of the proposal with the aldermen it represented. It was a way to bring more legislative participants into the picture. Once again I stressed the need for immediate action.

The next day I met officially with the Organization and Methods Committee to present the proposal for the new department. Not only were the regular members of the committee present, but also some aldermen who had a special interest in the matter. In addition, there were a number of representatives of citizens' groups, many of whom had been invited by my office to express community feeling on the plan. Although there were objections, the plan passed the committee by a vote of 4 to 2.

But the plan still had far to go to become a reality. I knew that there was opposition to the inclusion of the health and building code enforcement activities in the new department and could foresee aldermanic opposition to the plan because of these features. Part of my strategy was to give in on this flank, agreeing to leave out the code enforcement provisions for the time being in order to attain the major objective. But on July 22, the whole plan was put in jeopardy when a premature news story intimated that I had already selected Richard Perrin, Executive Director and Secretary of the Housing Authority, to head the new department.

It was true that Perrin had impressed me as a man eminently qualified for the job. He was a nationally respected professional in his field, much honored by the American Institute of Architects. Above all, I was impressed by his long administrative experience in the field of public housing and redevelopment. The difficulty, however, was that to some aldermen he was somewhat controversial because of his connection with public housing. I could see a threat to the entire plan if the battle centered around Perrin and if the aldermen were subjected to pressures simply because of a personality conflict. In response to the newspaper story, I stated that "it would be presumptuous to select a man before the council has created the department." But the situation was to resolve itself.

The president of the Common Council could not have surprised me more if he had fired off a cannon in front of my door when he publicly declared that Perrin should be named head of the proposed new department. He urged that I name the director first, and then let the council set up the department. Although I certainly felt that it was the mayor's prerogative to name the department heads, in order to move the matter ahead in the council I thought it tactically better to write the president that if he could get council approval and accord from the Development Authority and the Plan Commission by the following Monday, I would be pleased to name Mr. Perrin as director of the department. "Mr. Perrin," I noted in my letter, "has excellent qualifications, and I assume that you have received his consent." On Friday, however, the Common Council president was forced to report to the aldermen that Perrin was not interested in this manner of appointment. He immediately began to get a show of aldermanic strength in favor of Perrin—an attempt to convince Perrin that there was no solid opposition to his appointment.

By this time, too, all organized opposition to the department had folded. On Monday afternoon, July 31, 1961, the council approved the new department by a vote of 19 to 0. It had been a long and often anxious struggle, but the new department had finally been created after a shorter period of legislative action than for any other city department in our history. I had also made my point that the department had to be created before a director could be appointed, and I was free to make my own appointment.

On August 26, 1961, I announced the appointment of Mr. Perrin as acting director of the new department, and on October 5 he was officially sworn in as Director of the Department of City Development.

The department now consists of five major divisions: Administration, Management, Planning and Programming, Real Estate, and Technical and Maintenance. The Planning and Program Division "in many ways is the core of the department," as Mr. Perrin puts it. Through its current work section, it concerns itself with zoning, subdivision, and platting matters. Its long-range planning section works in such areas as preparation of the master plan, community renewal, traffic and transportation, and community facilities. A project planning section handles preparation of the workable program for urban renewal, specific studies and plans for public housing projects, urban renewal projects, and general renewal plans.

Mr. Perrin notes:

> It is in the work of these three sections that the virtues of the consolidation of the Department have been most apparent and possibly the most dramatic. In the past, we have literally had jurisdictional disputes between the planning staff of the redevelopment authority and the staff of the city plan commission. Redevelopment, as well as public housing projects, were frequently developed in a vacuum by the respective staffs of the two authorities simply because the city planning staff had given priority to other matters. By consolidating and unifying planning functions, all programs of the city are now handled comparatively and to mutual advantage with necessary priorities established by the director.

Among the residual problems that still remain is the question of consolidation of the three policy boards of the department. A study recommending consolidation has been completed, but as I write action is still pending.

The success of the department, however, has more than fulfilled our hopes for it. For planners, there has perhaps been a bonus that we did not anticipate when we first envisioned the department. As our planning director told a national convention after the department had celebrated its first birthday:

> To generalize about organization for planning on the basis of the Milwaukee experience to date, I would say it is clear that, in addition to all the usual inducements such as salary, fringe benefits, paid vacation, opportunity for advancement, and the like, planners need a feeling of belonging to the team, an understanding of the relationship between planning and development, a sense of direction toward achievement . . . in short, an attitude . . . an *esprit de corps*. This attitude is characteristic of Milwaukee's Department of City Development.

Initiating the Community Renewal Program

On the face of it, the logic of a Community Renewal Program as a prerequisite for urban renewal is incontestable. No one remodels a house until he has drawn a plan, looked at his bank account, figured what it will take to do the entire job, and decided in what order he will take on the various projects that fit within his means. What makes more sense than to take a look at the condition of the entire city, determine what has to be done, and work out a program of renewal commensurate with the city's present and anticipated resources?

Yet, in some cities, the idea of the Community Renewal Program has been rejected out of hand. My own experience in initiating our original plan indicates that more than idealistic acceptance of the logic of the CRP is necessary to get such a program across. Once again strategy and tactics are intertwined.

Early in my administration, I placed the initiation of the CRP at the top of my agenda. A number of factors entered into my decision, but high among them was the realization that projects were being undertaken helter-skelter, with little or no relationship to one another. It became clear to me that the solution to this problem was an integrated program such as that offered by a CRP.

As a first step toward this goal, I called a meeting of various city officials to discuss the subject. I outlined for them the purpose of a Community Renewal Program, pointing out that it would set out a positive program for city-wide renewal, conserving some areas and redeveloping others. I emphasized that our renewal efforts should be concerned with the total city and its total resources.

Although there was concurrence with the idea, no one knew exactly how to go about getting such a program. Someone raised the question of which was the proper federal agency to contact in the Housing and Home Finance Administration. There was general agreement, however, that the CRP would come under the duties and functions of the city's Board of Public Land Commissioners, then the title of our planning commission.

Contacts were made with HHFA officials in Chicago, and in October, 1960, the regional administrator wrote me that Milwaukee's interest in a Community Renewal Program was under consideration. Soon our preliminary application was in the mill. So I decided it was time to start laying the groundwork for approval in the Common Council. The first steps were educational: In speeches and conferences, I kept preaching the need for the CRP and explaining in a general way what it would mean.

In January, 1961, a resolution was sent to the Common Council directing the city to apply to the federal government for funds to finance the CRP. In the council committee considering the resolution, some aldermen expressed the first public rumblings of discontent. Despite this, however, when the resolution came up for a vote some three months later, the committee passed it by a 7 to 0 vote. The resolution called for an expenditure of $330,000, the federal government to pay two thirds of the cost. Three days later, the Common Council cast a unanimous vote in favor of submitting a formal application to the HHFA for the federal funds.

But the real battle lay ahead, when it came time for the council to appropriate the city's share of $110,000. I stepped up my educational efforts by making personal appearances, by utilizing the communications media, by contacts with other officials. Typical of the argument I made for the CRP is this statement from one of my speeches:

This (the CRP) is far more important than any of the individual projects that are continually being proposed to the mayor's office. The Community Renewal Plan will give Milwaukee a long-needed perspective in urban renewal. We can no longer cling to traditional virtues. Old World charm is not enough to meet the problems of rising costs and decaying tax bases that face cities everywhere. We cannot charm away problems pinpointing the need for more and better housing, the need for more roads and transportation and parking facilities and many other problems. We must act before we awake one day to discover the full package of troubles piled at our door.

Public appearances were tailored to fit the occasion, of course, but not a speech was made without some educational description of the program. It seemed to me that the more I could get myself quoted as strongly in favor of the Community Renewal Program, the better would be its chances for winning wide acceptance.

I followed the dictum that the program should take into account all residential and nonresidential resources, actions which could be taken with and without federal assistance, good urban design, knowledge of the economic potential of the city, population distribution, adequate housing for all income levels, financing, and necessary administrative and legal arrangements. My hope was that the end product would be a translation of all the required analyses and studies into a dynamic, time-phased program of interrelated public and private renewal, a program coordinated with the city's development prospects and trends. The basic purpose of the Community Renewal Program was to be (and now is) to expand the scope of local urban renewal from a project-by-project basis to the total community scale of need. I said that cities should be planning for the next ten, twenty, and even thirty years to make sure they will grow along sound, orderly lines.

About the middle of June I was in Washington, D.C., for the convention of the United States Conference of Mayors. I took advantage of the occasion to visit Robert C. Weaver, then administrator of the Housing and Home Finance Agency. Weaver assured me that cities with a community renewal program would be better able to get federal assistance, not only for projects currently on the boards but especially for future proposals.

In October, shortly after the Department of City Development was created, the HHFA came through with its approval of a grant for $220,000. Now the issue of appropriating the city's share of $110,000 was squarely before us.

A leading alderman won a delay for approval in the same committee that earlier had favored the CRP by a 7 to 0 vote. The members of the Common Council were apprehensive, as reflected in a statement from council quarters that I was "a mayor who was trying to build a power machine within city hall."

The main argument advanced against approval of the Community Renewal Program, however, came from the alderman who won the delay, an able council leader who later supported the plan. He contended, quite plausibly, that such a plan would place a stigma on large sections of the city by designating certain areas for different programs. His claim that the Community Renewal Program would "tend to scare the hell out of everyone" in many neighborhoods drew some support. It was time to get on with the work at hand, he said, and forget the planning.

The communications media thrived on the controversy. Objections to the Community Renewal Program were drawing more space and time than the good points. I stepped up my campaign, stressing that the program would emphasize preserving neighborhoods, not tearing them down.

My greatest fear was that rejection of the program at this point would be a lethal blow to the city's progress. It would be embarrassing and damaging to the city in its current and, of course, in all future dealings with the HHFA and the Urban Renewal Administration. At this point, I marshaled all the public approval I could find.

At a public hearing held by the aldermen, the city's most influential leaders in business, labor, and education appeared; heartening to me at this point was the discovery that my earlier campaign had been successful. A broad representation of community groups jammed the committee room, all wanting to be heard—in favor of the CRP. Meanwhile, I continued private conferences with the aldermen in my office, at lunch, and on the telephone in the evenings. The opposing alderman insisted all along that he had a sufficient number of votes to beat the plan, even on the morning of the Common Council vote. In the afternoon, he conceded. The vote in favor of the appropriation was 16 to 2. And he was not one of the two voting against it.

On February 1, 1965, I signed the Common Council Resolution approving our completed Community Renewal Program, one of the first to be passed by the legislative branch of any major city. President Lyndon Johnson, in his telegram of congratulations, said:

> The adoption of your Community Renewal Program shows the sincere desire to undertake vigorous action on a comprehensive scale to develop a more beautiful and prosperous Milwaukee. You have the additional honor of being the largest city in the United States to complete and adopt a Community Renewal Program. On this significant occasion in your city's history, please convey my best wishes to all those who have contributed to this bold, imaginative, and forward-looking action.

NOTE

1. Seymour Freedgood, "New Strength in City Hall," in *The Exploding Metropolis* (Garden City, N.Y.: Doubleday Anchor Books, 1958), p. 90.

five S for Strategy, T for Tactics: Programs within the Mayor's Office

The Division of Economic Development

On any working day of the week, a bright, well-dressed young man is likely to appear in the executive offices of one of Milwaukee's industries to announce: "I represent the city's Division of Economic Development. Is there any way in which we can help you?"

The reaction in the local business community has been one of utter disbelief. Some businessmen had never talked to a city representative before. If they had, it was to a bearer of bad news—such as a building inspector or a health inspector. The idea of the city's offering help instead of hindrance was unheard of.

As it turns out, there are many ways in which our young man can help. Businesses in a congested central city are faced with manifold problems. Frequently, some small action by the city—such as vacating an alley, changing parking regulations, or agreeing to a zoning variance—is enough to give a firm a new lease on life. The city also benefits by preventing many business losses that might otherwise take place.

This daily contact with industry is a practical symbol of the comprehensive economic development program Milwaukee has been shaping since 1960. This is not to say that the task is as simple as having a man call on industry. Our program, which is vastly more complicated than that, is still being refined, but we have made good progress in protecting and expanding our economic base, something every city has to do if it wants to survive. No city can successfully undertake more than its economy will support. All of our physical, social, and cultural goals depend on what we can pay for. The state of the economy determines the contents of our civic billfold.

The need for our local communities to do something about their economic futures interested me long before I became Mayor of Milwaukee. As a senator in the state legislature, I had taken an active interest in economic development legislation and had sponsored constitutional amendments to permit the state of Wisconsin to guarantee industrial mortgages. The amendments did not pass, but they did stimulate dialogue on problems of industrial development.

Economic development was therefore a major point of my 1960 campaign. I knew that whoever was elected mayor would face tremendous problems in this field. Milwaukee was and still is the ninth largest manufacturing center in the United States. It leads the world in the manufacture of diesel and gasoline engines, outboard motors, motorcycles, tractors, padlocks, and beer. It leads the nation in the production of work shoes, leather gloves and mittens, and saw and flour mill equipment. It is one of the nation's leading graphic arts centers and makes important contributions in many areas of capital goods equipment, including electrical controls.

But, in 1960, it seemed that this colossus of production was beginning to stiffen with age. Large industrial complexes had pulled out. Those that stayed behind talked negatively about the city and its potential. Communication between business and City Hall had deteriorated badly. That elusive quality economists call "business climate" seemed sour to many observers, including myself. The city was headed for trouble.

Until this time, Milwaukee had demonstrated little real awareness of the importance of its economic base. There was talk, of course, about its importance, but little backing of that talk with action. More often than not, the businessman got a hard time from City Hall rather than a helping hand. Too many bureaucrats seemed to act as if businesses were something to be discouraged or, at best, tolerated. This attitude, coupled with complaints about the Wisconsin tax system, undoubtedly contributed to sizeable industrial losses. Part of the problem, too, was that the city was not actively involved on the business firing line. Like most cities, Milwaukee had abandoned industrial promotion and recruitment to the local chamber of commerce. Unfortunately, the chamber now served a wide metropolitan territory, most of it more eager for new industry than the city of Milwaukee itself. Also, the chamber's agenda at that time did not permit an all-out industrial drive. That situation, fortunately, has been corrected, but the chamber remains flatly metropolitan in its outlook. The city, however, receives its main revenues only from those properties within its own political boundaries and must concentrate on maintaining its own economic base rather than that of the entire metropolitan area.

Although there seemed to be a wide gulf between my Socialist predecessor and the business community, he was not entirely unaware of the dimensions of the problem. He had an "industrial co-ordinator" on his staff, but there was no way in which one man could do all of the things that needed doing. As a consequence, I knew even during the campaign that this was a pressing problem. I called for a division of economic development in the Mayor's Office with a staff large enough to do the job. My proposal caused little more than a ripple and was not, as far as I could tell, a prime issue.

The lack of interest, however, did not undermine my determination to do something. After I took office in April, 1960, I began an intensive study of our general economic situation. My study was not only enlightening, but somewhat terrifying. I found that Milwaukee's industrial assessments had dropped more than $8 million from 1959 to 1960, a period when regional economic activity was generally healthy. (Our property tax assessments are made each May 1.)

This was bad enough, but I knew that a growing number of plants were housed in old or functionally obsolete quarters. Many manufacturing districts were depressing jungles of conflicting land uses—jungles born of years of bad planning and spot zoning. I found, for example, that less than 4 per cent of the city's industrially zoned land was actually used for industrial purposes, although up to 20 per cent had been set aside. The rest had gone into either nonconforming housing or commercial use. On a broader front, our general physical development was anemic, as symbolized by a downtown which many knowledgeable observers had written off as dead.

Worse than the outward signs of urban senility was the lack of hope among many of our top financial and industrial leaders for positive action by the city government. In private conversations I learned that many industrialists had decided to relocate rather than to expand their plants. Most of the time, the relocation was to be to one of the suburbs, which can offer short-run advantages to the industrialist, primarily in the form of initial lower taxes and low land costs. I recognized that these moves would not harm the metropolitan or regional economy, but the loss to our own city tax base could be catastrophic. There was no guarantee that Milwaukee wouldn't become a pocket of poverty inside a generally healthy metropolitan area.

So I really had very little choice. I had to mount an aggressive economic development program as part of a total development strategy. I had to get government doing those things it could do. More important, we had to find ways and means of attracting and stimulating more private investments.

In October, 1960, when I argued for the creation of a division of economic development before the city's Budget Examining Committee, I said, "A one-man operation in the field of industrial development is a thing of the past. . . . Every large city in the country is crowding us and the fight is getting tougher than ever." I told the committee that I was deeply disturbed by the city's declining industrial real estate assessments, while at the same time our city ranked high in most of the factors that make a city attractive to industry. "We haven't really spread our wings yet to sell what we've got," I said. "If the job is going to be done, I think the city is going to have to do it."

The aldermen were also disturbed by the situation, and were agreed that such a division should be created. However, they questioned the advisability of placing the division in the Mayor's Office. Several leading aldermen thought the division should be a regular city department. My view was that this particular function should be under the mayor where it could not only act with dispatch but would also be buttressed by the prestige of the Mayor's Office. One alderman supported my view with the argument that "The division should not have 21 bosses, the Mayor and 20 aldermen."

In November, the Common Council approved the new division by 19 to 1, the lone dissenter arguing that since the division would be in the Mayor's Office, the council would have no control over it. Initially, the division called for five posts—director, deputy director, economist, statistician, and stenographer—and a special Common Council committee was set up to work in conjunction with it.

Now we had the structure, but there remained the considerable problem of staffing. Personnel recruitment was (and continues to be) a major problem. No university I know is turning out trained professionals in this field, and the supply of persons with direct experience gained in other agencies is so limited as to be almost nonexistent. Although the work of the division calls for economists, purely academic courses in economics are not always as relevant to such work as they might appear on the surface. Some economic specialties, such as urban land economics, are, of course, extremely valuable, but I suspect that backgrounds in business administration are better for nonresearch positions. At any rate, the problem of staffing this particular division in its earliest days was one of the most difficult of my new administration. And I wound up making an initial mistake.

My choice as director of the division appeared well qualified on the surface. He had taught economics at a university and had had a short tenure as my chief administrator. My general concept of the division was of a research-oriented but flexible unit operating with a fully developed working rationale. As time went by, neither the rationale nor the working operation developed as I expected. There seemed to be little research except for what I myself ordered, and the accent seemed to be on public relations rather than on the substantive business of economic development. Obviously, there was a divergence of views as to what the economic development division should be. The issue came to a head when the division, in my opinion, failed to handle adequately the details of organizing the formative meeting of the Economic Growth Council set up to advise the division. At the last moment I had to take over the final details myself.

After working all night on preparations for the meeting, I took the presiding chair in the morning somewhat fatigued and in an atmosphere of tension. Once or twice the division director moved to get the floor, but I refused to recognize him since I did not want to risk a blowup in this important forum. Shortly afterward, on Easter morning,

1962, our divergence hit the headlines when the director angrily blasted the administration on a number of unrelated matters and announced his departure. As I look back on the event, the Easter proclamation appears to have been in effect an announcement of his coming candidacy for mayor of our city. (He ran against me in 1964, and was defeated.)

The departure of the division director settled one issue, but it left me in a delicate situation. Although I knew that the idea of the division was sound and that its overall goals were worthy, we were almost back at the start of our course toward those goals.

In addition, hints of impending danger to the division came from the aldermanic chambers. Some aldermen were thinking about taking the division out of the Mayor's Office. As I interpreted it, their motives were mixed: looking to the next election, some who pictured themselves as possible candidates for mayor saw a ready-made vehicle for harassment of the incumbent; some were piqued because they had not been included on the list of invitees to the Economic Growth Council meeting. (I learned the hard way that in city politics it is not enough to follow the practice I had followed in the state legislature of inviting only committee heads to meetings.)

The council talk involved reinstating the former director to head the division after it had been removed from the Mayor's Office. My information was that the move was to be initiated at the next meeting of the Common Council's Committee on Industrial Development, and I realized that if the movement did get off the ground, my administration would be embroiled in a long, embarrassing fight. And for the administration to lose such a fight would mean that irreparable damage would be done to its prestige. There was no question but that this was one of the biggest crises of my first term. Only after I had mustered every influence I could was the threat counteracted and the meeting turned into a routine affair.

But I still faced the critical choice of a new director. I remained convinced that only solid research and a well-defined rationale held the key to meaningful economic growth. I also decided that I needed long-term accomplishment more than immediate ballyhoo. I concluded that it was perhaps a mistake to think in terms of a rigid educational background in such a new field. If nothing else, my own experience indicated that I needed a nondoctrinaire approach to such a pioneering effort.

After considerable searching, I hired a newspaperman. He had had some earlier business experience, but the main reason I hired him was that he had a reputation as a hard-working researcher who could get a job done. The success of the division since then has vindicated my choice many times over.

The net result of my initial staffing error was the loss of almost two years of momentum. The new director had to start almost from scratch not only to build up a program, but also to assemble a fully qualified technical staff. The going has been on occasion, very hard, but in numerous instances the division has more than paid for its keep. The three individual case studies that follow should indicate how useful the division has been as problems—not only in industrial matters, but also on the broad economic front—have arisen.

THE POST OFFICE STORY

One of the few hopeful things I encountered in my first few months in office was the news that Milwaukee was in line for a new federal post office building.

The kind of priority we had was unclear, but the Post Office Department had considered several downtown sites and it seemed certain that the project would be undertaken eventually. I knew such a project would have a tremendous effect on our downtown area and awaited developments eagerly. The Post Office was negotiating with the Milwaukee Road Railroad for what seemed to be an obvious location near its downtown depot—at least, it was virtually a unanimous choice locally. It seemed the kind of project for which all I would have to do would be to show up for the groundbreaking. (As an older, and I hope wiser, mayor, I now know that there are no such big projects.)

At any rate, everything was proceeding about as normally as one could expect when one of our local congressmen began boosting a site about 4 miles from downtown, in a somewhat remote area. Both the downtown site and the outlying site were in his district, but the outlying site was more clearly identified with his district and was part of a huge Veteran's Administration hospital facility.

This talk of a new site began in the summer of 1962— just after the new division director had taken office—and began to build up during the autumn. The congressional elections were approaching. There was talk that the congressman was using this as a local issue and that he wasn't entirely serious. I was dubious because I know the congressman well and have a high regard for him, and I believe he was serious in his reasoning that his favorite site was better adapted for establishing a federal building complex on the local scene. The situation deteriorated rapidly, even though many observers were still not convinced that the congressman was serious. It finally became obvious not only that the new site had become a serious contender, but that the Post Office Department probably would end up picking it.

This was one of the gravest issues Milwaukee has had to face since I have been mayor. I say this because it was the community's will that the post office be built at the downtown site, as evidenced by the support of all the communications media and of influential local leaders.

The post office, as a building, was no longer so important; as a symbol it had become of vital importance. Few issues in recent Milwaukee history had so united frequently opposing groups. If the will of the community could be denied on this matter, there might never be a chance to develop such a display of spirit again.

Although I had been involved all along in the post office project, I had not, until this time, thrown all of my resources into the fray. Tackling it now, when all seemed lost, seemed at first like fighting cobwebs. The recalcitrant congressman was a man of high position in Washington, with extremely close liaison with the White House. He had to be handled carefully because I suspected—and still suspect—that he could have had his way if he had insisted on it. This made political tactics somewhat dubious.

After much thought, I decided that this was a fight that could only be decided by facts. I ordered the Division of Economic Development to drop everything else to work on the problem. I also appointed a distinguished citizens' committee to work with the division to compare the economics of the two sites. The committee included a powerful labor statesman, the chairmen of the economics departments of our two universities, two civic leaders, and four city experts.

This committee, with great help from the division, accomplished one of the most amazing research feats I have seen in some time. In less than two weeks, the committee published a 42-page analysis in which the two sites were compared from every conceivable standpoint. The downtown site was shown to be the obvious choice from every consideration of operation and service. Most important, the committee was able to demonstrate that the downtown site would cost about $500,000 a year less to operate than the outlying site.

The report achieved its purpose. Although the congressman attacked it as slanted, the Post Office Department either could not or would not raise a serious objection. It was clear that the merits of the case lay with the downtown site; only a political whim could be the basis for another choice.

But this was not the end of the struggle. Although the Post Office Department now began a serious exploration of the downtown site, many difficulties emerged. One was on the price of the land from the railroad. Another involved the relocation of the railroad depot, which also involved a downtown expressway project. And the sheer complexity of the project produced many snags.

I remained actively involved during this entire period, maintaining close contact with Post Office Department officials, including Edward Day, then Postmaster General.

We were beginning to think we were solving the problems when a new bomb dropped.

On March 21, 1963, headlines in the *Milwaukee Journal* quoted the Post Office Department as saying the downtown site posed "insurmountable obstacles." The department said that it and the Milwaukee Road could not get together on either the price for the land or the terms for relocation of the railroad facilities. We were given a sixty-day grace period in which to try to surmount the "insurmountable obstacles." The Post Office Department described the situation as apparently insoluble. After all the effort we had expended, we were back where we started. The post office was still a potent symbol. Losing the fight would cause a tremendous psychological letdown for everyone involved in the struggle—a letdown that might easily imperil many other worthy projects.

Fortunately, everyone was now inspired. The railroad found areas in which it could reduce its demand. The county and state, which had responsibility for the expressway construction, worked out arrangements to relocate the railroad depot. After many agonizing days, the "insurmountable obstacles" boiled down to a $250,000 gap between what the railroad had to have to relocate its depot and what it could get from all other sources.

Here was another hard decision. We stood to gain a $21 million post office, a new railroad depot (which later became a union depot, something the community has always wanted), and all the collateral development that would ensue, estimated to be as much as $50 million eventually. On the other hand, we stood the risk of being accused of subsidizing the railroad. In addition, there were a number of knotty legal questions as to how far we could go in tying down the project.

Again the Division of Economic Development sailed into the fray. Working with various city departments and the aldermen, the division developed basic information on what the city would gain directly and indirectly from the post office development. I made it my business to try to determine if there was any "fat" in the $250,000 figure. After investigation, I concluded that there was none. By this time, too, the division had, with the help of our Public Works Department, discovered areas for direct saving on such things as street costs and expressway ramps. The total amounted to more than the $250,000 asked by the railroad.

Fortunately, the Common Council had maintained a constructive attitude during this period and was prepared to act quickly once the facts were determined. Accordingly, on July 12, 1963, the council voted the funds, which technically were given to the county to add to the relocation payment to the railroad.

Since that day, things have gone smoothly. Construction on the new railroad depot—one of the few new depots constructed anywhere in decades—began on August 5, 1964; it was opened for business in August, 1965. Construction of the post office began in April, 1965. The benefits that were forecast seem as likely now to be forthcoming as they did then. More important, soon after the post office fight was settled, observers began talking of a downtown renaissance. Our "dead" downtown was now seen as making a comeback. As a result, several major private building decisions were announced.

I learned an important lesson from this project. No

modern mayor can cope with the complex problems which are likely to confront him without firm and rapid fact-finding. The Division of Economic Development gave me and the other public officials the facts we needed on this project—the kinds of facts no nongovernmental agency could have provided.

THE INDUSTRIAL LAND BANK

The Division of Economic Development has a functional assignment along with its staff duties. It must find ways and means of holding and increasing our industrial tax base.

In the case of Milwaukee's industrial land bank, I knew even before I was elected what had to be done. Like most large central cities hemmed in by suburbs, Milwaukee suffers from a serious shortage of the large, well-located sites industrialists now prefer for their sprawling one-story plants. As I mentioned earlier, an inadequate zoning ordinance has led to long-range dispersion of industrially zoned land to other uses.

Having recognized the problem, and knowing that there was no point in trying to attract industry if there is no place to put it, I campaigned in 1960 for an industrial land bank. The idea was to create an industrial land reserve which, by virtue of city ownership, would be impervious to rezoning and subversion to other uses. The land would be put into the bank for future use, but it would also be on hand for pressing industrial opportunities. I saw the land bank as a potentially important tool for creating jobs and adding to the industrial tax base.

As with the creation of the Division of Economic Development itself, I had little trouble in selling the basic idea. Any reasonable industrial development program is politically popular in this age of intense competition for new plants among states and cities. Of course there were some misgivings, legitimate and petty.

The legitimate misgivings centered about the city's intrusion into what had been the domain of private land developers—misgivings I also shared. I resolved them in my own mind by noting the recent industrial and industrial land history of Milwaukee, but I also was determined that the program be carried out with a high degree of prudence. After all, my basic purpose was to enroll the private industrial developers more firmly in our development cause, not to discourage them. The only point of the land bank was to permit land assembly which they could not undertake and to handle basic industrial opportunities beyond their capacity.

The petty misgivings were the kind which greet any new program: Once committed, the city would buy up thousands of acres of land and would be stuck with it. Certain areas or wards might be favored. Some land speculators would be "bailed out." Someone would make an unfair profit. Corruption was inevitable.

Such fears are common in our Milwaukee government. This is ironic in view of the fact that we have perhaps the most honest municipal government in America, and that is not an overstatement. Our problem in Milwaukee is that fear of potential irregularities paralyzes the will to act—but that is another story.

Despite the misgivings, legitimate and otherwise, the land bank passed unanimously when first presented to the

Common Council in November, 1960. An initial appropriation of $1 million was put in the 1961 budget.

But this was a hollow victory, because the Common Council had no intention of actually releasing the funds until a full-scale program was worked out. And the appropriation was made during the early days of the division, a disorganized period previously described, and no satisfactory program was offered. When the new director took office in June, 1962, one of his first assignments was to try to get the land bank idea moving. He quickly set about to develop a rationale. This was not easy, because such a program is largely dependent on opportunity and a sense of timing. Buying land that industry might eventually want to acquire is not like picking a library site.

I was heavily involved tactically during this period, helping the new director develop arguments that would appeal to various aldermen. The effort paid off, because we finally got a basic agreement on how the program should work.

Our sighs of relief were premature. No sooner had we laid out an acceptable program than we ran into a bonding problem. Although a state law authorized industrial land banks, there had been no test of its constitutionality. Similar programs had been declared unconstitutional in two other states, but those other programs had been far more sweeping. Nevertheless, Milwaukee's own bond counsel refused to approve the issuance of bonds for the land bank. This caused new misgivings among the aldermen, because Milwaukee traditionally has had the highest possible bond rating, AAA—a point of pride as well as a source of lower interest.

Many conferences ensued, but the bond counsel was

adamant. The aldermen were equally adamant about not issuing the bonds without approval. I tried to set up a test suit to establish the constitutionality of the state law but could find no takers among local financial institutions or elsewhere.

We were at an impasse. I frankly didn't know what to do.

Perhaps we should abandon the land bank, but I couldn't bring myself to do so. I had a feeling that I should keep trying. I began to ask if there were other ways in which we could finance the program, other ways in which we could establish the constitutionality of the law. Someone finally came up with the idea of borrowing the money from the city's debt amortization fund, a peculiar fiscal relic set up originally with the idea that the fund would eventually equal the city's debt and that it would then be used to retire the debt.

After much soul-searching, the city debt commission finally agreed to this internal borrowing arrangement. The aldermen again had misgivings because of the unique approach. More conferences ensued. Not until December, 1963, did we finally get the green light from the council to go ahead with the land bank on those terms and to start shopping for land.

It took time to prepare the shopping list. The fact that we were in the middle of the 1964 city elections—when the aldermen weren't about to hand new issues to their opponents—slowed the implementation of the land bank until immediately after the election.

Whether the Common Council would have gone along with the actual acquisition recommendations will never be known, because fate took a hand. Just as the division and our real estate technicians were completing their recommendations, the division ran into a hot industrial lead. Inland Steel Products Company, a subsidiary of the Inland Steel Company, was looking for an 80-acre site on which to build a plant to produce a new and exciting product.

Even in the throes of the campaign, the division began working with Inland Steel, which was also getting attractive offers from a number of suburbs. After much searching, Inland expressed interest in a site in Milwaukee if we could assemble the parcels and offer the land at a reasonable price. After studying the situation and conferring with me, the division decided to use the land bank as the tool. With the assistance of a number of outside groups and agencies, the division was able to tie down the site and make a firm offer to Inland Steel in less than two weeks.

The project represented one of the most complicated industrial cases ever witnessed in Milwaukee. With much effort and with much cooperation from the Common Council and outside groups, the Division of Economic Development carried it through to success. It was not only the largest industrial acquisition Milwaukee has had in recent years, but it was also the first time in decades that a large manufacturing complex had moved into the City of Milwaukee from one of the suburbs. (Inland Steel's main facility is in West Milwaukee.)

The division centered the first land bank acquisitions around Inland Steel, which ultimately wound up buying 85 acres. An initial plant of 150,000 square feet already has been built, but the eventual manufacturing space under roof is expected to reach 800,000 square feet, with total employment of about 800 people.

The city bought 183 acres altogether, leaving us almost 100 acres for our initial land reserve. Even after all our preliminary work, there is no way of knowing whether we would have gotten the land bank going without Inland Steel. There is strong feeling that the concrete opportunity was our catapult.

Since then, another $2 million has been authorized for the program, and we are moving to make it part of our permanent capital improvements budget. Some people still have misgivings, and I expect they will have until the program is more firmly established. We are, however, on our way toward creating a brighter industrial future for Milwaukee.

I learned something from the land bank struggle. If you believe in something deeply, don't give up even when it appears a lost cause. Hanging on, waiting for a break, can lead to success. I also learned that the division, with guidance, could be a powerful tactical unit as well as a fact-finding agency. Without its coordination of this very complicated endeavor, we would still be talking about a land bank, instead of operating one.

THE MILWAUKEE WORLD FESTIVAL

Besides its pragmatic fact-finding and coordination assignments, the Division of Economic Development has an important planning and basic research function. It must continually search for ways and means of improving the Milwaukee economy on all fronts.

Studies spearheaded by the division have literally covered the waterfront, dealing with such matters as riverfront beautification, downtown development, completion of our civic center (after decades of delay), encouragement of industrial firms to locate their headquarters operations downtown, assistance for firms displaced by expressways and urban renewal, and establishment of industrial renewal techniques; but I can think of no more interesting study than the one leading to a proposal for an annual world festival which would put Milwaukee on the international tourist map. The basic idea is to have individual companies and organizations sponsor appealing events, both cultural and athletic, which could be packaged for widespread promotion under the banner of the Milwaukee World Festival. The world festival also is a vivid example of the compelling power of a good idea.

The idea of a world festival developed basically from my awareness that Milwaukee, a delightful city in many ways, was not living up to its tourist potential. It was nourished by my visit to the Munich Oktoberfest while on a tour of Radio Free Europe and by an increasing appreciation of the diversity of Milwaukee's own charms.

I urged a study of the feasibility of a world festival in August, 1962, following the change of administration of the division. I was not interested in a "world fair," because I didn't think that the brick-and-mortar approach was right for Milwaukee. I thought that a series of static exhibits would not pull the whole community, with all of its potential, into play. I was also looking for more than a one-shot extravaganza. And while I was impressed by the Munich Oktoberfest, I knew that a Milwaukee world festival could not be an imitation if it was to succeed—that it must be adapted to Milwaukee's unique assets.

There was still a question of the practicality of the

project. How much community support would there be for it? How should the idea be developed? How much would it cost? How much would it return to the economy? To consider these and other questions, I proposed the appointment of a distinguished committee of business, labor, and civic leaders.

Even this simple organizational step, however, ran into rough opposition, primarily from an outstanding civic leader, a public relations representative of one of the city's breweries—an important economic interest. He had long planned a series of tourist events sponsored by his brewery alone. Who could blame him for fighting to preserve the field for his client? He conducted a skillful psychological war on me to convince me and others that the project was doomed from the start.

From our point of view, however, there was more significance to the festival committee than appeared on the surface. This was the first committee organized under the aegis of the new economic advisory board known as the Mayor's Economic Growth Council, a body that was designed to work with the division on a number of other important projects. If this project failed to get off the ground, the other proposed projects might also be in jeopardy.

For this reason, if for no other, I thought that it was important to convince the brewery that its best interests lay in joining the world festival concept. On the eve of the luncheon that was to launch the committee, the issue was still in doubt. During the early morning of the luncheon day, the aforementioned public relations representative called me. "You son-of-a-gun, you kept me awake all night," he said, "but we're in!" "That's good news," I said, "thank you." So, in the end, the luncheon went off as planned. Everyone who was asked to serve on the committee accepted his assignment.

There was still, however, a certain amount of skepticism about the project. After all, we were starting with little more than an idea. Several influential people expressed doubts at the outset about Milwaukee's capacity to handle such a project, but this was precisely the question I had asked the committee to resolve. I wasn't entirely wedded to the idea myself. All I wanted at this stage was a serious study of the potential of such a festival, but it was beginning to look as though even that would not be forthcoming. After several inconclusive meetings, the committee members decided they did not have enough information to make a decision. The proposal was returned to the division for further development, simply because there was no other vehicle available to handle it.

The division was in a quandary. None of its personnel had expertise in tourist events. And yet a plan had to be developed.

I told the division director that he had no choice but to pick the best minds he could find. He took me at my word. First, he held an all-day "brainstorming session" involving some of the most creative people in the community. He took their ideas and sorted out the ones that seemed to have the most potential. Then he named almost 300 people to 23 subcommittees to explore the various facets singled out for consideration. Among the subcommittees was a prospectus committee to hammer out the final plan.

The end product, released in the spring of 1964, was a

remarkable proposal for which many professionals in the tourist promotion field have expressed admiration. The plan calls for a variety of subfestivals—jazz, music, art, folk, and so on—grouped into a package with a number of existing tourist events in Milwaukee. It is the planners' conservative guess that the festival would attract 1 million people a year to the community and provide a boost to its economy of at least $10 million.

As of this writing, we are still working out the implementation of this long-range goal. A nonprofit Milwaukee World Festival Corporation has been formed and a professional director hired. Funds have been contributed by the state and county governments, in addition to those from the City of Milwaukee. Some still regard the plan as visionary, but more and more persons are beginning to see it as an achievable goal. Reaching it won't be easy, and it won't happen overnight. We could move more quickly, of course, but that would involve sacrifice of soundness and even risk of failure.

The important thing is that the community now has a comprehensive plan of action. Some of the suggestions contained in the world festival report already are being carried out. One group is seriously pursuing the creation of an amusement and recreation center similar to the Tivoli Gardens in Copenhagen, which parallels a suggestion made in the festival report. Several large firms are either getting involved in tourist events or are thinking about getting involved. Many aspects of the proposed festival are being pursued even as we are setting up the framework for an enduring institution.

Truly, in these days of struggles against blight, prejudice, and poverty, it is a pleasure to have at least one goal which involves joy. I know the members of the division, with their many day-to-day industrial headaches, feel the same way.

OTHER ACTIVITIES OF THE DIVISION

These three cases indicate how an agency giving exclusive attention to problems of economic development can be useful to the decision maker as he tries to evolve a total development strategy. But the division's main concern, of course, has to be with Milwaukee's industrial growth.

We look upon new industry as the frosting on the cake, well realizing that the batter is composed of expansion of existing industry. More than 85 per cent of almost any community's growth is likely to come from such expansion rather than from new industry. For this reason, the division spends much of its time working with established companies to solve their space and operational problems.

This work pays off. The 5,000-square-foot expansion here, the 10,000-square-foot expansion there don't seem like much individually—usually they aren't even reported in the newspapers—but they have a way of adding up. A lot of this kind of expansion has added up since the industrial assessment downturn in 1960—$26 million worth, to be exact, through 1964. This, I might note, was during a period when there were substantial and unavoidable losses as a result of public improvements. The same healthy trend has been noticeable in our commercial assessments (general, nonmanufacturing businesses), up almost $45 million during that same period.

Our field man has been helpful in encouraging many of

the smaller investments that can add up so quickly. He runs into a variety of problems—businesses are as different as human beings—and some of them require much imagination. We can't help in all cases: Sometimes we run into impossible situations; sometimes, like any of us, individual businessmen can be downright unreasonable. But we always try, and in large measure we succeed.

I should note at this point that under the Milwaukee form of government, it is almost essential to have the support of the local alderman for many of these efforts. It should also be noted that individual members of the Common Council have been most helpful in this bread-and-butter form of industrial development, since they share our concern for the community's economic growth.

But fieldwork of this nature isn't good enough if it is pursued only on the basis of current opportunity. In addition to trying to help specific industries, the field man tries to spot common problems. He files a report on each call. These reports, which remain confidential, are circulated among the division's research staff, where they are analyzed to pinpoint problems general to a neighborhood or to an industry or to a whole section of the city. These reports give us a better working knowledge of our economy, an appreciation of its diversity and constant change. More important, the reports have sparked the advancement of various proposals to correct conditions affecting more than just one firm.

I also like to think that this sort of effort is having a long-range, beneficial effect on the city's image in the business community. Talk is cheap in the industrial development field, but I think the growing number of companies we have assisted with their individual problems, both large and small, know now that we offer more than talk.

I think the division also has had a pronounced effect inside City Hall. It was frustrating to me when I first took office to find little evidence of real concern for the economics implicit in almost any program or service. The division's insistence that the economics of a given proposal be considered has inspired a new way of looking at things. More and more, it seems to me, our line agencies have broadened their horizons to think of the possible economic dividends from a given project. The Common Council also is beginning to demand information on the economic aspects of an issue before it makes a decision.

One indication of the increasing recognition of the division's efforts came in 1964, when the Common Council approved an increase of four positions to its staff. Altogether, with its clerical complement, the Division of Economic Development now has a staff of ten—small enough to be flexible but large enough to tackle complicated jobs.

With its increased staff and its preliminary organizational work completed, the division is beginning to concentrate more and more on industrial development, not forgetting that the amenities of city life (or lack of them) figure more and more in industrial decisions on location. Neither I nor the division believes that economic development can be a one-shot project; it must be a continuing program that truly recognizes the interlocked aspects of the private industry (both export and local service) and the public sectors of the city economy. In short, we agree with the premise that "in the broadest philosophical sense, the goal of economic development in urban areas is the improvement of human welfare."[1]

Although the arrears of decades force the division to concentrate primarily on pragmatic, action-oriented research in these early days, I have never lost sight of the need for a long-range plan. When the division's basic work is done, and when the crises diminish, I hope it will be possible to undertake a deep probe of the Milwaukee economy to determine, scientifically, its strengths and weaknesses. It is my hope that this study, which I have tentatively labeled an "economic growth potential analysis," will pinpoint our industrial advantages and disadvantages, as well as those lines of industry which offer us the greatest growth potential. This project is in keeping with my overall attitude that economic development should be approached on a "rifle shot" basis after thorough research. Fortunately, some of the more advanced urban economists are developing improved techniques for dissecting central city economies.

I also would prefer to have this study become a cooperative effort among city groups, business, labor, and the universities, since everyone has a stake in the results and should be committed to action on the results. For, although the Division of Economic Development has become a valuable mechanism in the pursuit of progress, it cannot operate in a vacuum. No community will grow or grow soundly if its various elements do not work together in harmony. This cooperative approach is at the heart of what I call the Milwaukee Idea.

Tactics of the Executive Budget Message

One of the most effective tools available for advancing a strategy of development and devising the tactics to implement it is the city budget. Here is the city's work program for the year with a dollar sign. If the municipal executive can influence the direction of the budget, he can, in large measure, advance his own broad goals of municipal development.

In Milwaukee, the mayor does not prepare an executive budget as is done in cities of the "strong mayor" type. Instead, a number of cooks are involved in the making of the budget pie. The Budget Department goes over requests with individual department heads, usually paring their requests sharply. The formal budget is prepared at hearings conducted by the Budget Examining Committee of the Board of Estimates, on which the mayor serves as chairman, together with the council's Finance Committee, the Comptroller, and the Budget Supervisor as secretary. Here is the main arena of the battle of the budget. Department heads can appeal the budget as prepared by the budget director, aldermen can gain a floor for their particular ward interests, citizens can gain an audience for any number of private pleas. The sessions grind on for weeks, and at the end a final budget is submitted to the Common Council as a whole—where, once again, there can be controversy.

Feeling that a strategy of public leadership required some executive direction of the city's budget-making process, early in my administration I started the practice of sending an executive budget message to the Budget Examining Committee. What is a mayor's thinking behind such a message? How does he attempt to advance his strategy in it? What tactics are involved?

The following section is one illustration. Excerpts from the 1963 executive budget message sent to the Budget Examining Committee before it began its hearings are followed by a commentary on the rationale involved.

The Message:

During the past three budget sessions, while dealing with short-run problems, we have also, more importantly, concentrated upon meeting our responsibilities to Milwaukee's future.

This year we must consider the budget, not only in terms of holding down the municipal tax rate, but also with the courage to complete the development programs already underway.

Step by step during the last three budget periods, we have allocated our resources to establish priorities for coordinated action on broad economic, physical, and social fronts.

Just as we have budgeted in the past to strengthen our development planning, our economic growth programs, our redevelopment priorities, our future housing conservation programs, our code enforcement to upgrade our neighborhoods, so now we must budget for the new agency which holds great hope for our social development—for our aged, our troubled youth, the disadvantaged. This agency is the Community Social Development Commission. It was formed to coordinate the allocation of our metropolitan resources to attack the social problems of the Greater Milwaukee Community.

This commission has now reached a point where budgeting is of importance—after the many undramatic months spent in bringing together the various governmental and private units necessary for its existence.

It is absolutely necessary that all the component units of the commission meet their responsibilities in providing a budget for the commission. I earnestly hope that the city government of Milwaukee will be the first to contribute to the budgetary strength of the commission. This should be our top priority since the city government of Milwaukee took the lead in bringing together the various agencies to form this landmark commission.

Another area in which I urge budgetary action is in connection with the Commission on Community Relations. As I did last year, I again urge the strengthening of our programming in this field.

This bi-racial commission is one of the most long-standing in the United States. Following the suggestion of its executive committee in 1960, and closely following the commission's prescription for membership, I personally made every attempt to give it as broad a representation as possible. The effort to fulfill this prescription commanded more time and care than any other appointive task of this administration. I am convinced that the members of this commission are citizens sincerely devoted to elimination of all forms of bias in the Milwaukee community.

However, the members of the commission are all volunteers with busy lives of their own. They need staff personnel to perform the research and the planning for programs to serve not only today's needs but also to prepare the way for tomorrow.

Last year I urged that a staff technician, designated as a program director, be added to the staff. I repeat this plea this year.

Beyond that, I feel that our primary goal should be to hold down the municipal tax rate as far as possible. In the long run, however, we cannot do this unless we concentrate on financial planning and smack harder than ever at the inequalities in the state-shared revenue structure.

Commentary:

One of the primary goals of the preceding passage is to point out important municipal goals that can be furthered by the upcoming budget, just as advances have been made by steps taken in the past budget.

The message begins on the high plateau of budgetary

thinking on which I wanted the Budget Examining Committee to act. But the message has a public audience apart from the members of the committee and the other aldermen, so I can also employ it as a forum for public education. For instance, there is a reference to a "step-by-step" process, which I happen to believe is a necessity in decision making in a democratic government. The phrase is inserted here mainly because I had pointed out previously that this is a process necessary in civil rights programming, and my political foes had set up a howl. Although some may quarrel with the repeated emphasis on a "step-by-step" process, I believe that people must be educated to the fact that there are no miracles in a government in which many must be persuaded before an inch of progress can be made.

Later paragraphs set forth my first choice of priority in the coming budget scheme. We have in prior years budgeted to bolster our physical development programs. This year I feel that it is important to provide the initial financing for the Social Development Commission of Greater Milwaukee. The commission, after long months of organization, has reached a point where it is ready for budgeting; now I hope to provide it with the staff to do the job of initiating and placing in focus the fundamental priorities for social progress in the community.

In dealing with programming in the field of human relations, I reaffirm my approach of the previous budget session, long before civil rights became an explosive issue. Once again I am carrying out my approach to decision making by improving my centers for initiation of choice. The purpose of the program director for the Commission on Community Relations is to search out ways to change the attitudes of those prejudiced against various minority groups; at present the agency is spending most of its staff energy "putting out fires."

The last paragraph is my political recognition of the citizenry's desire for official attention to economy. It is also my bridge to the next section, which takes up one of the most hidden, but most critical, issues of the city's future.

The Message:

The Effect of State Action on City Property Taxes

Few of our citizens understand that our local level of taxation in large measure reflects our treatment by the state in regard to state-shared taxes.

The City of Milwaukee must move to settle some basic issues which too long have been befogged by demagoguery, or swept under the rug by outsiders who demand service of us without reckoning with our ability to pay. It is noteworthy that the state government seems to view us as the fat goose that lays the golden egg. Others view us as a gigantic service machine for the metropolitan area, but one that is self-sufficient when it comes to paying the costs of running the machine. Others view us as an island for the poor and the underprivileged, at least partially surrounded by a sea of wealthy escapees from the city and its basic problems.

Since we are so many things to so many people, certain questions arise:

Is a disproportionate amount of our land going into tax-free institutions and public lands to service the entire metropolitan area? These institutions are good and necessary, but does a basic inequity exist to the city in this area because of disproportionate absorption by the city?

How does our per capita income and our per capita return from the state compare with other communities? in the metropolitan area? in the state as a whole?

What new state aids should we fight for, if any, to rectify

inequities that exist in the relationship of the central city and its problems to the state?

Present state-shared tax formulas sharpen the differences between "have" and "have-not" municipalities within the state. The "haves" get the larger slice, while those subsisting on half a loaf are handed crumbs.

This has resulted in disproportionate property tax rates.

The city too long has been entrapped in a maze of conflicting opinions about its limited resources. The question is whether our resources should be used for the betterment of the "have-nots" of the state when we may be among the "have-nots" ourselves. Certainly, there are "haves" which should be carrying a larger share of the cost of state and local government.

The broad assumption that bigness is richness must be factually challenged. To challenge this assumption, a comprehensive analysis is imperative. I, therefore, recommend:

1. That our Citizens' Commitee on Revenue Distribution be supplied the funds to carry out the analysis. This committee has already demonstrated its ability in the past.

2. That the committee be enlarged to utilize the many talents of and give full representation to our metropolitan area.

3. That at a later date a full-time legislative representative be selected to present the analysis and such recommendations that the common council and the mayor may approve to those who will join our efforts for equitable tax distribution.

Commentary:

A fundamental decision is reflected in this section. I feel that now is the time to open my attack on the state's revenue distribution setup. I know that this is a long-range fight; I also know that the fight has never before been made in the manner in which I intend to wage it. I have decided, after much consideration of alternative vehicles (such as the Comptroller's Office or the Bureau of the Budget), that the Citizens' Revenue Distribution Committee, a small body that has been almost anonymous, is ideally constituted to carry on the battle. I would beef up that committee after the analysis mentioned here is made. I would find out who our allies in the state might be—the "have-nots" as opposed to the "haves"—and would then, for the first time, seek to get the personnel to carry out an organized program of attack upon state revenue problems. As a beginning, I propose a "full-time legislative representative."

Notice that in the choice of language ("the fat goose that lays the golden egg," "surrounded by a sea of wealthy escapees from the city"), there is no attack on the state or the wealthy suburbs directly. I do not want a direct fight at this point.

The presentation moves on to consider the local economy in the next section.

The Message:

The City's Economic Outlook

One area in which we lack precise knowledge is that of our own economy. All of our plans, in the long run, are at the mercy of that economy. All of our plans, in the long run, should be aimed at improving that economy.

One difficulty is that very meager information is available in the Milwaukee city economy, as distinguished from the metropolitan, regional, state, national, and even world economies. Yet our own economy is the ultimate measure of the taxes we will have available for vital government services and programs to promote progress.

This does not mean that we can take a provincial view of our economy and regard it as absolutely distinct from the other economies. All are linked and must be viewed in relation to one another. However, we can do little, if anything, about those other economies, and we can do something about our own. The health of the other economies does not necessarily guarantee continued health for ours. If we do not continually exercise care, we can become a pocket of poverty inside a booming metropolitan, regional, and national economy.

This is why I have urged an intensive and completely realistic economic base analysis of Milwaukee. We must pinpoint the real state of our economy, understand how it came to be, and identify the forces of change now at work. We cannot continue to operate in the dark in a day when rapid change demands quick and exact response from government. We must have a solid foundation of knowledge on which to base the very considerable improvements we have made not only in the budgetary process but in many other areas of government. I, therefore, recommend that we make a token initial appropriation for "seed money" to finance such an analysis which will provide an indication of the city's willingness to participate in this project.

As for the economic conditions which face us in this current budgeting period, we seem to be in a period of relative stability. Locally, we have the irony of probably the greatest building boom in the history of the city coupled with the loss of taxable property to the expressway program and other public works as well as diminishing values in some areas because of the withering hand of blight.

We think that our gains will continue to exceed our losses, and that is better than many communities have been able to manage. The situation, however, points up the grave need for more and more economic development activity and every penny spent constructively in this field will be worthwhile.

Commentary:

In the original draft, this section was almost a throwaway near the end of the message. In deciding the final points of emphasis, I gave the section a higher priority, even though I realized that it dealt with an intermediate-range proposition and was not likely to produce tangible results during the coming year. It did, however, point up the necessity for continued development of another center of civic strategy—an economic development program.

Looking over the budget situation, I envision the flight of industry to the suburbs and the loss of middle- and upper-income groups, which under the Wisconsin tax structure weakens our base for shared income taxes. There is the nightmarish question: How long can we cope with the rising costs of the service demands on the city without an enrichment of the city's revenue base? The ultimate answer can no longer be sought in a higher property tax rate, but must come either through new or renewed economic areas adding to the assessed value of the tax base or producing more income that can come back to the city in the form of shared taxes.

In addition, without a clear notion of the local economy, the city can do no substantial financial planning. Little or no thinking has been done in the past on the economic underpinning of the city's future; decisions have been made largely on the basis of political expediency rather than on the rational basis of economic logic.

Here again, I am endeavoring to reinforce my center of future decision making. I have already organized a Division of Economic Development; now I am calling for the methodology—the economic base analysis—that will lay the groundwork for more scientific economic planning at the municipal level and provide a benchmark against which to test financial decisions.

One of the important areas for financial decisions is in the capital improvements budget, which is taken up in the next section of the message.

The Message:

Capital Improvements Financing

Our city government is making additional progress in capital improvements financing. Because we planned well and last year switched some of our continually recurring capital improvements programs to a cash basis, substantial savings are falling our way. This year—for the first time in many years—we will be able to cut the net cost of principal and interest on our outstanding debt.

I favor continuation of this program, and I recommend that a portion of the sewer construction financing now be switched to a cash basis.

I realize that additional borrowing may be necessary to complete the civic center or to finance other projects delayed from previous years. These are proper uses of borrowing and must be expected in the march of civic progress. However, our program of cash financing for recurring capital improvements should be expanded regardless of special one-time borrowing needs.

I also hope that we will continue our policy of advance planning of capital improvements. It is not only good planning, but it puts the city in a position to take advantage of grants in aid offered by the federal government as part of anti-recession legislation now passed by Congress and operating on a limited scale.

The capital improvements program is not only a means of providing necessary municipal facilities for our citizens. It also can be an effective weapon in fighting recessions if our planning is sufficiently far advanced to enable rapid translation of plans into jobs and work opportunities.

Commentary:

There had crept into the Milwaukee municipal financing picture a false notion that it was good policy to finance regularly occurring items on a bonded basis. In previous years, I had successfully urged a partial reversal of this policy, and street programs were switched to a cash financing basis. Now I am carrying the process a step further, asking that the sewer program go on a cash basis. The goal is to try to reduce debt over the long run and to keep borrowing allocated to the "big hump" civic expenses.

The reference to capital improvements planning in connection with the federal government is simply a "look ahead" reminder that we always face the possibility of recession and that the city must be prepared to receive federal help and accelerate its own program.

In the next section attention is focused on one of the thorniest items in any budget session.

The Message:

Our city employes have shown, and I am confident will continue to show, a high level of efficiency, enthusiasm and competence. The city has found through long experience, just as private industry has found, that the greatest economy in the wage area is a fair wage. It should, therefore, be our goal to continue to provide city employes with fair treatment and a wage and fringe benefit level which is comparable to the prevailing level in the community.

One consideration is always with us. And that is the difficulty we have in filling certain positions. Here, increases in wages over and above the average granted to other employes may be required to assure adequate municipal services. In this, the economics of the marketplace may have a louder voice than any other.

In these matters, as in others, we must keep one eye on the over-all tax rate and the impact of the Legislature's tax limits for operating purposes.

As you know, we asked the current Legislature to raise our operating tax limit to a more realistic level, not only because of the demands of growth and change, but because of the fluctuating nature of many revenues which must be considered in determining the final operating tax rate.

The Legislature raised the limit slightly, but then promptly wiped out almost half of the increase by "skimming off" part of the municipal share of income tax receipts. The Legislature also capriciously enacted an amendment apparently requiring the common council to adopt the operating budget by a two-thirds vote.

Actually, the amendment is so vague that I have requested the City Attorney to give us an opinion.

Regardless, the net result of legislative action has been almost no improvement in our operating budget limit. This is crucial for two reasons. One is that we must contend with automatic wage increments, new services or positions already granted, rising costs of some supplies, materials and services, increased fire protection charges, two additional elections, and increased workmen's compensation costs. Secondly, we expect only a small increase in the property values on which we base our taxes.

Accordingly, we have no choice but to ask those who demand major new or additional services or proposed higher spending to tell us where we can get new sources of revenue.

Commentary:

This passage might well be subtitled: "The mayor walks a tightrope." I am seeking to give encouragement to the wage negotiation representatives—the finance committee —without giving any basis for a complaint that I am interfering with the negotiations. In other years, the members of the committee had felt that my predecessor had weakened their position in bargaining; I want the committee to feel secure, but at the same time want it understood that the city is bargaining in good faith. I believe in bargaining in good faith, but I also believe that the welfare of the taxpayers must be kept in mind.

I praise city employes out of appreciation for their contribution to a high level of municipal performance. At the same time, I stress the need for wage equity. Again I bring up the subject of the legislature to show the strictures it places on city spending, this time to impress the negotiating committee and the department heads with the fact that there is a legal barrier to uncontrolled tax increases.

In the last paragraph, I call on those advocating new "major" expenditures to recommend new sources of revenue. By implication, I do not include in "major" expenditures my previous new spending recommendations, which are minor in terms of dollars, although their social effects could be enormous.

It should be noted at this point that legislators seem to be reluctant by nature to move in the social areas, no matter how small the sum involved. A multimillion dollar sum for a physical improvement will be approved more easily, it seems, than an authorization for a pamphlet dealing with sociological problems. If, in this budget message, I were recommending many new items of expenditure, the legislative body would balk at the sociological areas. But I have the optimum time for my presentation. This is due in part to the atmosphere created by the civil rights demonstrations. Here I have the happy circumstance of a choice coupled with events that support the choice.

The Message:

Improvements in Budget Procedure

This year we are expanding the performance budget concept to include additional bureaus within the Department of Public Works. The actual performance reporting and accounting necessary to make the figures more meaningful in terms of services is underway in three important pilot areas.

As yet, of course, comparable figures for a series of years are not developed. However, progress is being made and when this program is fully developed it will present to the Budget Examining Committee, our citizens, and the department heads themselves, a better view of municipal operations—a detailed picture that should show areas for both large and small economies.

The performance budget will, in the coming year, be applied to the Bureaus of Forestry, Street Sanitation, Garbage Collection and Disposal, and Plumbing Inspection. Together with the Health Department, the Bureau of Traffic Engineering, and the Central Board of Purchases, these seven agencies will place a major segment of the municipal budget under the performance budget format. This program will, I hope, continue to be extended wherever practical to other areas of city operations in years to come.

This year for the first time the Budget Examining Committee will have available another fiscal instrument I previously recommended to assist our review. This will show in individual columns on budget worksheets the amounts requested to (A) adjust for a workload change, (B) improve the level of service, (C) provide new services, and (D) meet special one-time costs. This should provide a useful tool in analyzing budget increases and in achieving major economies.

In considering capital improvement requests, the Budget Examining Committee would do well to seek the answers to the following questions I proposed last year in connection with each project:

1. What is the relationship of the proposed project to the welfare and progress of the entire city?

2. How many citizens will be helped by it and how many citizens will be harmed or inconvenienced if the project is not constructed?

3. Will it replace a presently outworn service or structure, or is it a new venture?

4. Will its construction add to the city's operation and maintenance budget, or will the property be largely self-supporting?

5. Will it add to the value of the area and thereby upgrade city property?

6. Is its estimated cost within the city's ability to pay?

The city's budget is only sound when it is based on sound information. We have made important progress toward developing more detailed and useful information than ever before. We must maintain our momentum.

Commentary:

In previous years I have stressed the need to transfer the city's budget from an object-of-expenditure basis to a performance or program basis. Since it takes several years to make the transfer complete, I am again pointing up the worthiness of the operation and the need for patience. The procedural achievement will realign the entire emphasis of spending and will enable the budget makers of the future to evaluate the city's operations with more adequate information.

The questions concerning the capital budget represent in Milwaukee a new standard for testing the evaluations of the capital improvements committee. They follow a recommendation of the Municipal Finance Officers' Association.

The message was communicated in excerpts through the radio, television, and newspaper media. Then it was read to the budget examining committee, where three of the five aldermanic members applauded it—a rare reception for such a document. On the Saturday evening following the reading before the committee, I took a revised copy of the message before the people in a television broadcast, largely because I wanted broad public understanding of my choices in order to gain, if I needed it, some public support in the days ahead when the Common Council would decide whether or not to concur with the "end of the beginning" of my strategy of development.

NOTE

1. John H. Nixon and Paul H. Gerhardt, "Urban Economic Development," *Annals of the American Academy of Political and Social Science,* XXXLII (March 1964), 40.

six Enrollment and Power

In the interest of creative leadership, one of the most important things a mayor can do for his community is to analyze his own sources of influence and his capability to produce results—in other words, his power. This self-analysis is seldom undertaken since he becomes so preoccupied with substantive decisions that whatever estimates he has of his influence are too often derived ad hoc and by intuition.

The mayor can evolve a most carefully thought out strategy and can be most determined to exercise responsibly his institutional leadership, but he will fail if he lacks an understanding of one important facet of power: the necessity of guarding his public standing. The creative leader can become so absorbed in his institutional programming that he can allow his public standing to be eroded and, thereby, his creative leadership to be hamstrung and his political future to be jeopardized.

He must be sufficiently balanced to cope with everyday events and crises and still push his long-range programs.

This is not an easy task. The problem is further complicated because the Mayor's Office, like any other institution, has only so much capacity. In the exercise of his creative leadership, the mayor would be wise to take inventory of his influence resources, and to expend them only when the benefits outweigh the costs. For a Mayor's Office can absorb only a limited number of problems, and with every expenditure of energy in one area, it has that much less to use in another area. The office must expend its energy where it will yield the biggest return and always with a flexible timetable, because the institution may suddenly, of necessity, become a "fire-fighting" machine to protect the very root of its leadership, its public standing.

Discussion of Power

Fundamental to the success of an institutional leader is his understanding of the concept of the "game" environment in which the public leader moves. "The interpretation of the event will be largely determined by the game the interested parties are principally involved in," says Norton Long.[1] This is the key to how much influence he may have to exert as he strives to exercise his positive policy leadership. It is also the key to guarding his most fundamental source of power—his public standing.[2] The game of some opponents is to destroy his authority, prestige, and status, and for some reason—perhaps because it is a nasty subject—there is little recognition that much of the time of the mayor is frittered away beating off inimical political gamesters in an effort to guard his standing.

A new mayor soon feels like a man sent to fight Goliath

with his bare hands. The accumulated and mounting problems of the city crowd into his office: problems of change, growth, and age. His city is absorbing some of the country's ill-fed, ill-housed, ill-clothed, and those unaccustomed to the ways of the city. Resources at the disposal of the city cannot deal with these problems. He faces problems unheard of a few decades ago, and as these problems increase he must maintain old services while initiating new ones.

As a candidate, he focuses on the attainment of office and what he wants to accomplish. As mayor, he must focus on means. The election victory envelops him with substantial public standing and, with the feeling that the election is now over, he begins to plot his course for the future.

Then he finds the election is never over. He discovers that he lives in a constant stream of published attack, spouting at times from all directions. These attacks are most often designed by political gamesters to weaken his public standing. Some of them—after thus striking—wind up calling upon the mayor for leadership. Usually an attack is well prepared. The attacker has the initiative, the choice of time, and the opportunity for extensive preparation. The mayor, if he is to respond in the medium conveying the attack, must do so quickly or his answer loses timeliness. It would be great fun, like counterpunching in boxing or tackling in football, except for its effect upon the processes of creative leadership.

At the moment his policy agenda may be heaviest on one issue, in comes an attack on two others. So progress on his agenda must be halted and his physical and emotional energy diverted to decision making on how to deal with attack. He must push aside his planned policy objectives (unless he can entwine them with his reaction). Many a central city mayor goes to his office in the morning with a major developmental problem on his mind only to encounter some harassing action that may absorb his attention that day and often for days to come. As Wallace S. Sayre says, "The morning's news stories and editorials more often set the day's agenda for the mayor and his associates than do the mayor and his staff."[3]

Never was this better illustrated than in the "letters of resignation" episode, to be detailed later in this discussion. The marshaling of the mass media to "cover" the stories was immediate and insistent. The mayor was deluged for comment on each of an endless stream of new "facts." On a single day—at the height of the coverage—the mass media had 13 reporters demanding the mayor's time for a variety of questions throughout the day and into the night. The mayor had become a "news source" exclusively.

While text writers glibly ridicule a mayor's inability to establish his own agenda in the face of such demands by the mass media, doing so in situations such as these is impossible. It is impossible because of the obvious political risks involved, particularly the very real risk of permitting the creation of an erroneous image which will follow the mayor into the polling place. With the stakes so high, a mayor has no alternative but to put his attention to methods of proceeding. Programming, projects, planning, administration—all must be pushed aside.

The time and energies of the mayor in these situations must be directed toward careful direction and control insofar as possible of the image being given the public. Although he is immediately on the defensive, he must strive to take the offensive to project the decisiveness that marks him as a leader. The how of this is not easy, but no matter what energies he must expend, the creative mayor cannot ignore the war of attrition by political gamesters upon his public standing.

This diversion is in contrast to another conflict with his agenda that is entirely legitimate. This is the civic agenda: the interests of those who, having a specialized interest and desirous of getting his attention turned to a specialized problem, may try to get a priority from him through pressure. This diversion is part of the agenda of his institutional leadership. The war of attrition, however, must be repelled, because it erodes the public standing the mayor needs in his attempts to gain policy objectives. His prestige enters into the reaction of people who decide how to respond to his requests. This includes the Common Council, the state legislature, his city departments and civic groups. His public standing is a major source of influence with them. When he is unimpressive in his public standing, then his opportunities for progressive leadership are reduced. And while he may not get the desired response even with high public standing, lowered prestige strengthens and augments resistance, whereas high standing tends to check it.

How is a mayor's public standing assessed? People watch for signs in the press; they listen to television and radio comment; they sample the attitudes of social and economic groups and organizations. They are affected, in other words, by the institutions of communication and the local society. There are, of course, special linkages in specialized groups. In Milwaukee, the reaction of aldermen is important for those who deal with City Hall. The families of city workers take their cues from the city worker. And all those who have articulate voices on public matters, such as the labor unions and the political parties, also influence others.

The mayor's constant problem is that too many expect results concerning things that are beyond his jurisdiction and his authority. In one term, I find, he can run into all the following problems, none of which is under his control: two municipal strikes in a high-wage city; a recession; civil rights demonstrations; a long, wide-ranging John Doe investigation of alleged police corruption. These are matters that produce innumerable complications, some of which he cannot avoid, and all of which tend to depress the community. But he can keep free of a great deal of trouble by understanding the different games and by avoiding becoming enmeshed in them. If he is trying to exercise strong institutional leadership, he must be doubly on the lookout lest he (as I did in the "letters of resignation" controversy which follows) unsuspectingly blunder into the middle of other games, and thereby court political disaster.

Because a mayor cannot meet all the demands upon him, he must determine what expenditures of his energy will yield the best results. His basic problem is to stay within the range of activity that suits his institutional programming, to find ways to control his agenda, and to place his agenda in the public focus in such a way that sound institutional leadership is protected and effective. This is the objective of his science of leadership. His art consists of finding ways of riding events that will project his agenda while not becoming enmeshed in the games of others. If the mayor is to guard his public standing when such events as the "letters" arise, his only recourse is a general attempt to clarify his role to the public, in particular to restate his objectives and relate them to the event. In his creative endeavor, he often fights the problem of inattention. When he can command attention, he had better make the best of the opportunity and, when possible, relate his total efforts and programs to the event.

The Case of the Letters of Resignation

On January 11, 1962, the *Milwaukee Journal* headlined: "Lag in Appointments Revealed by Report." The story said that the mayor had responsibility for filling 312 positions and that there were 69 vacancies or expired terms, although it acknowledged that 32 of the vacancies were minor. In fact, the positions were not empty; people were carrying out their roles until formal appointment was made, a customary practice.

The article went on to allude to previous troubles in appointment matters. It said:

> Maier ran into a nightmare last June when he appointed ——, an insurance man, to the safety commission. After the appointment was announced, it was disclosed that —— [the appointee] had lost his driver's license for two months in 1960 for speeding.

Concern over this "nightmare" had caused me to check out my appointments more carefully, and because I lacked the power of automatic removal of key appointees without "cause" involving complicated legal procedures, the safety commission case had prompted me to take letters of resignation in advance from some few important appointees—

27 out of 215 appointments made up to the time the practice hit the headlines.

No newsman asked me directly about the practice for almost a year and a half although, I am informed, at least two regular city hall reporters and at least one television editor knew about it. Actually, a combination of converging games vaulted the matter into big print: political opponents were seeking to embarrass the administration as municipal elections grew nearer, and a news-oriented John Doe investigation into alleged crime and corruption in the police department was under way. I had been concerned about reports that the morale of the police department was low because of the great publicity surrounding the John Doe. Patrolmen were said to be taking a verbal roasting on their rounds and their children were said to be targets for snide remarks from schoolmates. The chief had invited me to speak to his men, in three shifts, on December 11, 1962. I did, and among other things, I said:

> We—and I mean by that the hundreds of thousands of your neighbors—well know that we have a police department with an unmatchable reputation for law enforcement, criminal investigation, and general protection of life and property.
>
> We know that your integrity—and that of the thousands who came before you—has kept Milwaukee the safest, most crime-free metropolitan center in the nation. And I shall try to hold those responsible who may falsely malign you.
>
> So don't be disheartened if some few people appear ready to charge all 1,800 of you with the misdeeds of a handful. That's human nature. You just remember that there are hundreds of thousands of us who know of your dedication and hold you in the deepest respect.

I certainly did not regard that morale builder as any threat to the John Doe, an investigation I had endorsed.

Although our city charter does not give the mayor control over the police department, it did seem to me that morale was a problem for which I was properly accountable. Therefore, I was startled when a reporter told me as I emerged from the final session with the police officers that the judge conducting the John Doe was storming in his chambers because he said he had been told I was attacking him and his investigation. The newsman's report seemed so unlikely that I laughed, but not for long. When I got back to my office, I was confronted by another reporter, one making his reputation on Doe disclosures. He asked pointedly about my "letters" policy. I candidly admitted the policy and was careful to point out that I had made no secret of it.

The headlines the next morning portrayed a great revelation based upon my admission. The story featured a reproduction of what purported to be a copy of one of the resignation letters. It was not the form letter, but it closely resembled one furnished me by an election commissioner who had given me his own letter.

Remembering from my state senate days the passage of a bill making it a crime to lie to a newspaper, I informed the district attorney that someone was lying to the newspaper in furnishing a false copy of a resignation "letter." The newspaper, of course, refused to disclose its sources, but the district attorney was able to trace the copy to an assistant city attorney (a friend of the election commissioner) who had been one of two major opponents in the 1960 election. This brought out the Republicans in force. Perhaps the most ironic part of this was criticism by the Republican chairman of my use of a law passed by a Republican legislature and signed by a Republican governor. The district attorney outlined the facts and suggested I drop the matter. My purpose had been served.

The uncovering of the role of the assistant city attorney and one-time campaign opponent was a much less happy event, as it turned out, for he immediately called upon the John Doe judge to investigate. The judge, still smarting over my talk to the police department, was more than happy to accommodate. It developed that he already had the false copy subpoenaed.

Although the subsequent stories made it clear the Doe judge was investigating only my "letters" policy, my involvement was against a background of previous stories of many months touching upon alleged corruption and the antics of prostitutes and gamblers. The judge ultimately backed away from his investigation when the chairman of the fire and police commission, a retired circuit judge and retired law school dean, who had been the judge's teacher, publicly reprimanded him. The controversy died as I had planned—after I made a television address—twelve days after the hullabaloo started. In that address I covered my institutional objectives, pointing out that, in contrast, they had not received the attention of this fiasco. And I announced I was discontinuing the policy because the city attorney had ruled the letters invalid.

During this tumult, only two of the host of stories were aimed at trying to get a perspective. In one, it was pointed out that Presidents and governors had used the policy and that spokesmen for the U.S. Conference of Mayors and the American Municipal Association did not regard the policy as unique. Both spokesmen backed "strong" mayor forms of municipal government. In the other story, two political scientists from Marquette University decried the public furor as unjustified and made a reasoned argument for more power for the mayor. Without more power, they said, the mayor could not discharge his charter duties, and added:

> The day is now upon us, or soon will be, when the odds will be too great. We need to choose now between giving adequate power to an elected official who will be responsible to the people, or facing the prospect of a city government that wallows ineffectively in the problems of urban disintegration. In the light of the above statement, we strongly recommend an unfettered mayoral appointing and dismissing power over his major subordinates. . . .

After my television speech, the paper which had initiated the matter said: "We are inclined to think that this whole affair, in spite of its rather frantic headlines and its copious treatment in the news columns, may turn out to be a good thing for Milwaukee." And I was heartened by the following remarks in an editorial from the Racine *Journal-Times*, a paper that had been observing the matter from a neighboring Wisconsin city:

> Whether or not you like Mayor Maier's rather direct methods, however, it must be said that he has pointed up one of the fundamental weaknesses in Wisconsin's form of government, the so-called "weak executive" system. . . .
>
> Why should a state or municipal executive have more power? Because he has responsibility, and power should always match responsibility. Politically the governor and the mayors are held responsible for the actions of administrative agencies during their term of office. If the whole administration looks good, the governor or the mayor looks good; if, on the other hand, things go bad they are blamed. That is perfectly proper if the executive has the necessary control over the policies and actions of his adminis-

tration. He should neither be praised nor blamed if he does not have the power.

The strange sequel to all this came when the same election commissioner whose advance-resignation letter triggered the controversy became the subject of grave charges of hate-peddling. He had been quoted as saying that the late President Kennedy was a "traitor" and with passing out literature labeling Senator Barry Goldwater a "kosher conservative." I was besieged from all quarters, including several of the commissioner's former defenders, to fire him out of hand. The demand for dismissal, of course, ignored the very stringent limitations placed by state law upon my power to remove election commissioners. In fact, I ran into criticism for attempting to employ what little powers I did have.

Enrollment

Entwined with the mayor's ability to protect his public standing—and in a sense dependent upon his success in doing so—is the mayor's ability to enroll support and gain public backing or consensus for his objectives. It is at the heart of all his efforts, and it is central in the STEPP of the D-STEPP formula.

Enrollment, as used here, is the attempt to gain support for a program or a project or a point of view from representatives of groups. In its broadest sense, it means the effort to enroll the citizenry behind the same wide conception of community that is involved in the mayor's strategy of leadership. His success or failure in enrollment depends upon his solutions to his problems of communication, particularly the problems of attention or inattention, as well as his choice of means of communication, his manner of communication, and the energy that he can afford to put into acts of communication.

To be successful in his efforts to enroll, the mayor must keep in mind an attention scale. The physical audience he has in front of him at ceremonial functions is at the top of the scale. It is a small section of his mass public, but it gives him an opportunity to enroll. He must do so within the context of his forum. His audience at an award dinner by an Italian society scholarship fund, for instance, expects a testimonial to its efforts. He can, however, at least raise questions that relate the subject of the affair to his own objectives of office; he can draw relationships and outline his program. These forums have the prime attribute that there he will get attention.

To attract attention for the major objectives of his institutional programming through the mass media, he must create or ride events; otherwise his production cost in time and energy for a particular effort may be too high. Timing is extremely important. It will be abortive to undertake a major effort at a time when other events are crowding attention.

Television is a fine medium for the communication of institutional objectives. But it takes great preparation and is best used if the mayor can ride an event that will gain attention. Radio is another excellent medium for transmitting the weekly roundup of important activity. Material is easy to prepare and deliver for this medium, and if collateral effort is made to build the attention of a select audience of listeners through special mailing, the results can be appreciable.

A mayor's most frequent daily contact is with the newspapers. Here his dilemma is similar to that of the newspapers themselves, and attention is not the critical consideration. Edward C. Banfield and James Q. Wilson, in *City Politics*, have pointed up the newspapers' dilemma in treating civic affairs in depth: (1) cost, (2) time—matters that cannot be explained or analyzed quickly do not interest the newspaperman, (3) space limitations, (4) preoccupation with what is unique rather than what is typical. The authors say, "Particular circumstances of time and place are 'interesting'—generalizations are not. But it is only in the terms of the general that serious analysis can proceed."[4]

Mr. Arville Schaleben, executive editor of the *Milwaukee Journal*, in an address to the Milwaukee Chapter of the American Society for Public Administrators on October 12, 1962, underscored the basic philosophy of a good newspaper. In doing so, he, too, touched upon the dilemma of the newspaper that creates a dilemma for the mayor:

> The citizen reader must realize that we newsmen feed into his mind that which is subject to human judgment at every turn. This poses to us a terrific responsibility, greater than the capacity of the human mind to exercise with infallibility. Our press has the faults of our people—and their saving virtues. . . . We have made errors, we have abused our privilege on occasion, we have used doubtful judgment. . . . Yes, the modern newspaper is the source of attitudes which comprise the public mind.

Against this background, a mayor's efforts to enroll become a steeplechase. He must ride a temperamental horse over many hurdles to keep his important policy considerations in public focus. But it is a race which must be run. For where he lacks the formal powers of command—and this is in most of the areas of his leadership outside those of housekeeping—his power is simply the extra weight in persuasion or bargaining that his position gives him. And he had better be an expert in the use of this vantage point.

What possible guidelines are there for the development and use of this expertise? Sound decision making requires consultation where the limitations of time permit. Here the leader is really trying to build as much high-level consensus as possible among interested parties. Much of the affliction of the office arrives when the pressures on one front cause a failure of communication on another. There is much current research on local power structures, on who wields or possesses power in a community. One might ask, "Where is this research leading? Is it leading to a process of municipal leadership? Can the reinforcement of leadership through the employment of influential people and groups be placed upon a scientific basis?"

Common sense tells a wise leader that he must enroll those interested in a given objective. The intensity of their enrollment lends strength to his position. The impressiveness of their position and their character adds to his strength. Legislative and administrative decision makers like support and the reassurance of backing for a position. When such support is absent, insecurity arises and delay results. The reorganization of the Department of City Development and the establishment of the Social Development Commission, for example, had substantial enrolled backing which expedited the work.

So long as he enjoys a reasonably high standing, the leader will find the support to add weight to his case, if he concentrates on searching out the stakes for those involved in any situation. These stakes may be financial, academic, or civic; they may involve prestige or a sense of duty—in other words, they may be whatever motivates men. Most often, the leader's greatest failures occur when he fails to make such a search.

The crucial question before the Mayor's Office at any time is, "Who is interested in what?" In the case of the letters of resignation, if I had been able to quickly select and impanel important local persons into a task force, interested in and qualified to judge problems of authority, destroyed the letters, and asked the task force to evaluate and report with recommendations on my dilemma, I might quickly have relieved the pressure with good grace. If the "who" is not obvious at the time of the event, the event may move too swiftly for the mayor to take effective action in the area of enrollment of potential allies. Nobody can tell him when the moment for calling forth his support has arrived; he must rely largely on his intuition for this purpose. But he should recognize that the greatest problem of democratic leadership is to anticipate the problem areas and the types of negative public attack that may eat away at an executive's constructive efforts. He must consider the methods of possible opposition and gear his efforts to mustering the support he may need at the moment he chooses to do battle.

The Milwaukee Idea

In a number of ways my administration has sought to enroll all sectors of the City of Milwaukee in civic programs.

There are, of course, the formal appointment powers of the mayor, which permit him to name a fairly substantial number of citizens to various boards and commissions. If he knows the makeup of his city, this power is an important tool for providing widespread representation on the official city roster. In addition, the various segments of my strategy of development have presented additional opportunities for citizen involvement with our physical, economic, and social development programs—on the Citizens' Planning and Urban Renewal Committee, for instance, or the Economic Growth Council of the Division of Economic Development, or the various subcommittees on social matters attached to the Social Development Commission of Greater Milwaukee.

For some time I had referred to our city programs, together with their citizen enrollment, as the "Milwaukee Idea." In my second Inaugural Address in 1964, I dwelt at some length on this idea of involvement and the "Milwaukee Idea." I pointed out that during the past four years, "the Milwaukee Idea has succeeded in setting up programs and organizations to deal with the basic social, economic, and physical problems of the community. During the past four years, the Milwaukee Idea has enlisted the talents and support of labor, business, the professions, and the universities to work towards the solution of our problems."

This was not mere rhetoric. This coming together of various segments of the community to work for a common cause was to my mind one of the main achievements of my first four years of office. It seemed to me that this second inaugural message was a good occasion to call on those enrolled in these broad efforts to push a step further.

Among other things, I sought to enroll more support in the crucial battle for resources for our city.

The Milwaukee Idea, I said, "calls for a recognition by all those who make demands on our resources that they must help us find ways to replenish those resources." A recommendation of the same order had been mentioned in my executive budget message of the year before (analyzed in the previous chapter). Now, however, the reference was more pointed:

> It's time that they not only point out what Milwaukee should do, but also recognize what Milwaukee can do within its presently limited resources.
>
> While the City of Milwaukee will continue to meet its responsibilities, we can no longer afford the game of let's pretend:
>
> The suburban pretense that we can shoulder all the burdens laid upon us without adequate compensation—and this includes the weight of the expressway system and the disproportionate weight of tax-exempt property;
>
> The local critics' pretense that we can do everything at once, without insisting on priorities of action;
>
> The metropolitan pretense that we can meet our problems—the great problems of growth and change—without also taking steps to enlarge our resources.

Many who were in one way or another enrolled in the Milwaukee Idea were not citizens of the City of Milwaukee, but had important stakes in the city and in its future. Although, strictly speaking, the message was addressed to the people in the Common Council chamber, its echoes ranged far, simply because the message was an "event" and one that was usually thoroughly covered by communications media. The occasion was ripe, I thought, not only to point out the dilemmas of the city government, but also to call upon those who had interests in the city, but lived outside it, to help the city solve those problems.

Consequently, I proposed some transfer of functions from the city to the county government to spread their costs more equitably over a wider tax base. I also proposed that the county assess and collect property taxes for the various taxing units located within its geographic boundaries, since the county government encompassed a larger area and only about one third of the Milwaukee city tax bill was levied by the city's Common Council. I knew that these changes would be difficult to achieve immediately, but there was fertile ground for discussion and the minimum gain would be wider understanding of the inequities involved in the present system.

Other inequities, I pointed out, lay in the state's system of shared taxes and state aids which, in effect, help the low-tax communities to maintain lower taxes without giving sufficient relief to high-tax communities. As an example of this inequity, I cited the case of one Milwaukee suburb in which the per capita cost of municipal government was $72 more than the cost per person in the City of Milwaukee. Yet, because of the present shared-tax formula, the tax rate in Milwaukee was 262 times greater, despite the fact that we have a lower cost of government.

My main argument was that if we corrected some of these inequities, Milwaukee would have more room in which to conduct its developmental programs—the long-range efforts to put us on a better footing in the future. Among other things I called for greater citizen enrollment in our neighborhood development effort and the opening of service centers in the neighborhoods to provide citizens with the advice they need for helping to preserve their neighborhoods. With greater citizen enrollment I hoped that we could bring about greater citizen understanding of the city's overall planning goals and better expression of citizen desires.

This recommendation is in keeping with my belief that effective action must be preceded by dissemination of information to all who will be touched by that action. The establishment of neighborhood goals and standards and the holding of neighborhood meetings go far toward the eventual solution of some of the social ills of the big central city. Although there is always the chance that neighborhood groups will also become centers for dissension and impossible demands upon the city government because of the primarily narrow view of some of them, overall the interaction of social forces will be healthy in that it will compel planners always to be aware of people. Furthermore, efforts toward conservation cannot possibly succeed without participation in decision making by the people affected—except in terms of code enforcement, which is minimal in conservation efforts.

Again, speaking of our efforts for economic development, I said:

> As I see it, our top priority in the next four years is to go on a "war footing" in the nation-wide battle for plants. We must step up our defenses to stop or at least reduce the pillaging of our existing industries and, at the same time, begin mounting a strong counteroffensive aimed at capturing some new plants ourselves.
>
> This is a community problem and calls for a community-wide

effort. Government can do its part but it cannot win this war alone. This is a job for not only the citizens and their elected representatives but for organized labor, the Milwaukee Association of Commerce, the Greater Milwaukee Committee, the Milwaukee Development Group, the utilities, the railroads, the universities, and even the communications media.

This was an appeal for enrollment directed to those who had a specific stake in a specific problem. Tied in with it was a request for additional staff for the Division of Economic Development and for cooperation in developing an economic growth potential study.

Again, I appealed for enrollment of a wider segment of the community in the fight against discrimination and for the development of human resources:

> It is time for a wider recognition of the responsibilities of everyone in the metropolitan area toward meeting the complex problems of social change.
>
> Neither the city nor the metropolitan area can afford this waste of human resources. The city, as I say, is moving to meet this problem, but it cannot do it alone.
>
> There must be wide acceptance of minority groups throughout the metropolitan area and to this end I call on each suburban unit to set up a human relations commission to work for better understanding in each community. Let us work together on a problem that concerns us all.
>
> And separate from the problem of human relations, there must be the full utilization of the total Milwaukee community's resources to meet our social problems. There must be widespread backing of the Social Development Commission of Greater Milwaukee.

There was an important appeal for enrollment to those who could help the city win its fight for a better portion of state aids and shared taxes. This issue is an important part of the battle for resources that the city needs if it is to develop the Milwaukee Idea. In this effort, I admittedly put on the hat of an educator. Strangely, it is in this role, so often equated with mental serenity, that a mayor will many times find his greatest frustrations because the sound and fury of his political opponents and the impact of other events often muffle him. The great dilemma of leadership in a large urban society is not initially, as some may think, that there is lack of two-way communication. Often there is not even one-way communication between the elected leader and the electorate. With this disadvantage the mayor cannot begin to convince his city that there might be something more important than (or, at least, equally as important as) the pothole in front of the driveway or the inconvenience of the traffic jam or dilatory garbage collection.

This particular message, with its emphasis on enrollment in the Milwaukee Idea, was an effort to break through the attention barrier toward a broader realization of the total scope of municipal government. The reaction from the press and many influential people was good. Most citizens, I think, liked the part about a better tax break from the state. Some were especially interested in one section, others in another. By and large, though, more and more people were becoming aware that this city had programs under way and that these programs were moving ahead on several fronts.

NOTES

1. Norton E. Long, "The Local Community as an Ecology of Games," in Oliver P. Williams and Charles Press (eds.), *Democracy in Urban America* (Chicago: Rand McNally & Co., 1961), p. 372.

2. Richard E. Neustadt, *Presidential Power* (New York: John Wiley & Sons, 1960), chap. V.

3. Wallace S. Sayre and Herbert Kaufman, *Governing New York City* (New York: Russell Sage Foundation, 1960), p. 669.

4. Edward C. Banfield and James Q. Wilson, *City Politics* (Cambridge, Mass.: Harvard University Press and the M.I.T. Press, 1963), p. 323.

seven *The Nondeferable Decision*

Whatever else may be required of the modern mayor, one of his chief responsibilities is that of decision making. There is no way to avoid this responsibility, for even if he refuses to make a decision, he has to decide to refuse. Effective or not, the ostrich is trying to solve a problem when he sticks his head in the sand.

Decision making in the sense in which I use it here does not refer to dealing with those long-range plans of the municipal leader's own choosing for the ultimate solution of city problems or the greater development of urban resources. Decisions of this type, which I prefer to call *choices*, are involved in his strategy and tactics. Here I am referring to meeting what might be called the urgent or nondeferable decision. It concerns the problem that arises from action initiated outside the mayor's agenda, which clamors for his attention *now*, and whose resolution lies squarely in his hands. This process might be called deciding the "other-directed" problem.

The literature of decision making, of course, runs the

gamut of approaches to this process. Here we have James Menzies Black telling us there is no school for decision makers.[1] No one can tell you how to make a decision; there are no rules as such. On the other hand, Edward Hodnett tells us that "Problems . . . are much alike in structure and they respond to much the same techniques of solution."[2] Both from study and from experience, I'm inclined to go along with Hodnett. In fact, I used his approach in 1960 when I set out to develop a formal guide to decision making in the Milwaukee Mayor's Office.

This guide does not make decisions automatic. It is not designed to be a mechanical device but is intended to be used with flexibility. It does not pretend to relieve the executive of his decision-making responsibility. However, it is a handy guide outline for the executive himself, or a useful reporting form for his staff or assistants.

I was already acquainted with some of the short models of approach to this fascinating process of making up one's mind, beginning with the classic steps described by John Dewey: (1) perplexity—an awareness of the problem, (2) analysis and clarification by observation and reflection—definition of the problem, (3) consideration of different solutions or working hypothesis for solution of the problem, (4) verification of the solutions chosen.[3]

John Millett's summation of the elements entering into the process was useful, particularly his insistence on the use of broad concepts of human and physical behavior to predict future developments,[4] as was Frederick Randall's analysis of the process in terms of a personal creative approach. Randall describes the process as: (1) sensing (recognizing a problem), (2) preparation (gathering data pertinent to the problem), (3) incubation (mulling over the data, the subconscious activity which precedes an insight or inspiration), (4) illumination (recognizing a possible solution), (5) verification (testing proposed solutions).[5]

All these sources led me to construct my own proposed model for a mayor's decision-making process in the context of decision making previously described. In outline form, it is this:

1. The available facts must be gathered for identification of the causes of the problem. The answer to the question "What has occurred?" leads to the question "Why has this occurred?"

2. Following this point of identification of the problem, assumptions may be made based upon intuition and judgment.

3. Resources must be analyzed to find a means to the solution.

4. Based upon fact, assumption, and resources, alternatives are selected, each built upon hypothesis. While subjectivity must necessarily be involved, it is possible to designate the combination of desirable objectives that each alternative seems to offer in an effort to quantify alternatives.[6] This may be the basis for a table of comparison of alternatives.

5. Each alternative must be examined in terms of the "foul-up" factor,[7] the conflict that it will provoke. It can be stated as a rule that some people will react to one or another variable of the decision. If the total of adverse reactions is overwhelming, the decision is not likely to stand in a democracy.

"What you might take over from the scientist," Hodnett states, "is the habit of approaching problems in an organized way."[8] This organized approach is what I attempted to gain from the formal guide to decision making.

The formal guide used by the Mayor's Office of the City of Milwaukee is known as the M-25 (Mayor's Office form 25), which is illustrated on pp. 156–159. (For an illustration of the actual use of the form, see the Appendix.) It

---

STAFF REPORT*   OFFICE OF THE MAYOR

(Note: Where space is insufficient attach   CITY OF MILWAUKEE
an appendix)

I. PRELIMINARY ANALYSIS

A. Problem Identification:

    Suspend judgment until presentation is complete and you are sure you grasp the whole problem and have identified the real problem, rather than the apparent one.

Date of report_____

Common Council file #_____

Analyst_____

Target date for action_____

Originator_____

B. Description: Problem Situation and Its History (Outline):

    1. *Make your summary brief, accurate, and clear.*

    2. *Use words that define the problem exactly; make sure there is no ambiguity in the terms used.*

    3. *Include what is known; point out what is unknown and must be found out.*

C. Scope of Analysis (Financial, Legal, Organizational, Administrative Questions):

    1. *It may be necessary to group factors as:*
        a. *Factors controllable by you.*
        b. *Factors subject to control of others.*
        c. *Factors subject to chance.*

    2. *Ask yourself such questions as: What is the budgetary impact? What are the potential beneficial or nonbeneficial effects on tax and other revenues? What legislation exists or may be required? What existing agencies can handle the problem? What administrative plans have been made on the project or proposal?*

---

* This is a specimen of the formal guide to decision making referred to in this section as the M-25 form. Within each section is shown the instruction for its completion.

D. Facts Assembled (Financial, Legal, Organizational, Administrative, etc.; give source):

	Relative Weights		
	1*	2*	3*

1. When you cannot check facts directly, be sure you thoroughly question the source. (The complete Report Guide lists a number of sources for factual material, such as municipal reports, legal guides, department reports, libraries, checking to see what is done in other cities.)

2. According to your opinion of their relative importance, assign relative weights to the various facts you have gathered.

3. Does it appear that there is an overriding decisive factor in your analysis? If so, what is the consequence of its presence?

E. Assumptions:

1. Ask yourself: What have I assumed to be true in this situation? Is it true? How do I know? What other assumptions may be true? What can I do to test their reliability?

2. Challenging what is believed to be true about a problem that has not been solved is often the quickest way to find the reason why it has not been solved.

3. Errors of assumption include assuming facts that aren't so, inferences that aren't logical, universal opinions that are incorrect.

4. The skilled problem solver has to develop an automatic skepticism, especially about "obvious" answers and dogmas.

F. Alternative Solutions and Consequences:

1. Standard practice for all problem solving is to list all the possible alternatives before making a decision.

2. When you are faced with a problem that offers only an unpalatable solution, if you can find one other possible solution or alternative, you have changed the problem in a fundamental way.

3. If the problem turns out to be a true dilemma, which is the lesser-evil course?

4. Consideration of consequences, secondary or direct, is a big part of problem solving. Set up criteria to test results. Sometimes probable success is easily demonstrated. Sometimes it can be demonstrated only by elaborate technical proof. Sometimes it can be judged by opinion only. Yet you have not thought out your attack on a problem until you have estimated what the consequences of each effort to solve it will be.

---

* 1. Very great importance. 2. Important. 3. Least important.

II. EVALUATION   F. A. R.

A. Public Relations (Groups or Individuals Affected):	Alternative # 1	2	3	Relative Weights*
1. Evaluation is the product of the analyst's judgment and the result of opinion research involving respective groups.				
2. Estimate the relative effect of the various alternatives on various groups involved: also, list the groups according to the way you rate their comparative importance.				
3. Typical groups to be considered are: (a) Those with immediate pecuniary or economic interest; (b) Those with immediate legislative interest; (c) Those with broad civic or community interest; (d) The general public.				
B. Official Relations (Groups or Individuals Affected):				
1. Have you sounded out sentiment of those officially involved such as the Common Council, city, county, state, or federal departments or agencies which may be affected?				
2. How does this decision accord with previous decisions by those concerned?				
3. If a reversal of policy of others is involved, is the issue significant enough to warrant the change?				
4. Have you listed and weighted opinions of those involved?				
5. Which alternatives will involve the greatest net gain or the least net loss in our official relations?				
C. Press:				
Have you consulted previous news stories on this matter? What editorial positions have been taken, either recently or in the past?				

D. Recommendation:

A recommendation is essentially "a counsel as to a course of action." It should be held to essentials and be clear and definite and based on conclusions supported by your prior analysis.

* 1. Most important. 2. Very important. 3. Important.

E. Action Advised:

> 1. List the procedural steps that should be taken to carry out the above recommendation.
>
> 2. Include such things as the timing of the announcement of the decision, the manner of its announcement, and the order in which the steps should be taken.

---

presents a logical structure of information and presentation. The municipal executive can use it alone, but it is also an excellent form for persons reporting to the mayor (and sometimes it even proves to be a good system for finding out how much people know or don't know about a particular problem). It can be used in council with department heads, a staff aide, or outside experts. It gives those working on the report flexible but automatic guidelines and a check-off system for preparing their analysis. It speeds up the process of decision making because it organizes and streamlines the approach. It is a guide to thinking through the problem, and it is consistent with the rule of our office to reduce thought to writing for the sake of clarity, conciseness, and time-saving.

The M-25 report calls for the assembly of facts, identification of problem areas, laying out of assumptions (and disengaging them from facts—an amazingly difficult feat for some people whose credentials would indicate that they could do this with ease), selection of alternatives, and calculation of consequences (including research and testing of the possible social reactions of different individuals and groups to the different alternatives).

In use, the initial presentation of the M-25 has never been accepted as final, nor have the recommendations been received without some further modification. In the case of the Brown Deer decision, to be discussed later in this chapter, the reports were turned back five times to the staff group before the final choice was made. In the case of the 72nd Street library veto, the rudimentary M-25 analysis first presented to the mayor implied a recommended course opposite to the one he finally followed. But, as in all cases, the use of this reporting form enabled the decision maker more immediately to get the feel of the essential problem, to test assumptions, to calculate consequences, and then to enter his own set of institutional values as he made his final choice.

In addition to producing a process for schematic problem analysis, the M-25 is a fine guide for group discussion and testing of recommendations of the original analyst. It enables the one charged with making final decisions to spot errors in presentation quickly. But, for me, the greatest value of the M-25 approach to schematic decision making has been its paring of the vast amount of time and effort required to gain a clear perspective of all the facets of a particular problem of the type illustrated in the two cases that follow. One case shows the M-25 evolving; in the other it is fully applied; but in each case the completed analysis allowed me to comprehend rapidly the full significance of the problem, examine the alternatives suggested, and apply my own knowledge of the facts and personalities involved to arrive at my ultimate decision.

The instructions entered in the specimen M-25 deal with factors which, in my opinion, are essential for arriving at a rational decision. Proper reporting on the guide can free a municipal executive from the necessity of searching out, in every instance, all the relevant factors and permit him to weigh more fully the importance of each. Use of the M-25 guide makes possible a decision based on a thorough analysis without inordinate expenditure of time in attempts merely to grasp the essentials of the particular problem. Thus the M-25 has helped me, as chief executive of the City of Milwaukee, to cope with these nondeferable decisions, while at the same time forging a long-range program for the total development of the city.

In my opinion, the system has passed the only test that ought to be made of it: it has proved a successful guide in the decision-making process. It has enabled the various decisions to stand well in the face of attack. It instills confidence that the choice is as good as can be made within the limitations of what Millett has called "bounded rationality," the limitations of human beings to respond to reason. The greatest testimonial to the process that I have received was in the form of a comment of an alderman on the 72nd Street library veto, who softened his opposition to my position after the message was delivered with the remark that the case for veto made "too much sense."

The 72nd Street Library Case

Sooner or later almost every mayor is going to find himself embroiled in a controversy which pits partisan interests against those of the city as a whole. This happened to me early in my first administration. The cause of all the shouting was a building usually associated with quiet tones—a library. The nature of the decision that had to be made in this case set me on the road to instituting a formal guide to decision making in the Mayor's Office.

In the fall of 1960, the budget review indicated that Milwaukee would have to reduce its appropriations for capital improvements if it wished to avoid an unreasonable increase in the tax rate. One of my recommendations was that the Budget Examining Committee strike out a $400,000 appropriation for the construction of a branch library on Milwaukee's southwest side, leaving in only the $75,000 allocated for purchase of a site.

Because a site had not yet been purchased for this particular library, it was not likely that construction could be started in 1961 anyway. The Budget Examining Committee approved the request. And then, I found, in such little teapots great tempests are brewed. On the very same day that the Budget Examining Committee took this action, a Parent-Teacher Association from the southwest side of town began circulating petitions asking for a reinstatement of the library building appropriation in the budget. Within a few days, more than 3,800 signatures had been secured, a number sizable enough to make an alderman take notice.

The petition, however, did not ask that the library be constructed in the southwest area named in the proposed appropriation. Instead, it asked that it be built on a site which had previously been purchased by the city at South 72nd Street and West Oklahoma Avenue.

The Library Board of Trustees had recommended the advance purchase of this site for several reasons. For one, it was available; for another, the price was low compared with what it would probably be at a distant date when it would be needed. At the time the site was purchased, the Library Board noted that eventually two libraries would be required in the rapidly developing southwest portion of the city. It made it clear, however, that the first and most important of these would be a replacement for the rented library quarters in the populous area around South 43rd Street and West Oklahoma Avenue. Only after that need was met was construction to proceed on the South 72nd Street site. Funds for the library there were not even projected in the current six-year capital improvements program.

Later our office research indicated that at no time was the South 72nd Street library seriously considered for immediate construction by any professional staff of the city—not by the budget, public works, planning, or capital improvements committees, nor by the Library Board. It was evident that the funds originally included in the 1961 budget were earmarked for replacing the inadequate facilities some 29 blocks to the east.

Unfortunately, the impression had been given that the South 72nd Street library was scheduled for early construction. The PTA petition cited, among other things, that the South 72nd Street property had been owned by the city since 1959 and that the site contained a large billboard with a picture of a branch library and the statement that a library would be built on that location (no date specified, however). Later in our research, it appeared that the sign had been erected by the library under pressure from the previous alderman who was, unsuccessfully as it turned out, seeking reelection at the time.

Some attempts were made to clear up the confusion. The head of the Neighborhood Services Division of the library stated publicly that the South 72nd Street structure had not been planned until 1967 or later. At PTA meetings in the South 72nd Street area, he tried to explain the priority need for the library in the South 43rd Street area. On October 18, 1960, a resolution was introduced in the Common Council to direct the city real estate agent to negotiate for a library site to replace the South 43rd Street facility. The resolution was referred to committee for study.

During the month that followed, pressures mounted to reinstate the appropriation for a branch library building on the southwest side. Three days before the adoption of the budget, the Common Council stated its intent to budget $200,000 for a new branch library "on the southwest side" which would be "built in 1961 if possible." The council expressed hope that it would be possible to put up the building during the forthcoming year. It struck out, however, a specific reference to the South 72nd Street site which was contained in the original resolution submitted by the aldermen from the area.

Since the amended resolution specified no site, I was generally in accord with it. But there was still the budgetary consideration, and I suggested that the appropriation be in the form of an authorization for a bond issue rather than cash. The council went ahead with a cash appropriation on the same day the budget came to me for approval. Since there had already been some slicing of the original appropriation and there was no mention of the 72nd Street site, I did not feel that at that late date a budget veto was in order. The main fight, it seemed to me, was to maintain a city-wide rationale in this whole matter of library planning.

The resolution calling for purchase of a site in the South 43rd Street area was still hung up in the Common Council committee. On November 22, the committee met and postponed action on the resolution, largely because of the urgings of the local alderman. This was a setback, but it was also a gain. The question of proper library site planning was beginning to come to the fore, and the city librarian was directed to submit to the council an explanation of the library's priorities for branch buildings.

The question was again paramount at a (rare) public meeting on the matter held on December 13 by the city's Capital Improvements Committee. The committee heard from the library staff, citizen representatives, PTAs from the affected areas, and local aldermen. The outcome was a vote to retain the first priority given to the South 43rd Street library. The Library Board went even further. On December 16, it not only upheld the priority but specified that the new library should be built in the approximate area of South 35th Street and West Oklahoma Avenue.

Not unexpectedly, the well-organized PTA groups in the South 72nd Street area brought out their heavy artillery, firing their first salvos of criticism at the city librarian for not favoring their preferred location. Other volleys were fired at the mayor. City officials felt the full weight of angry protests from letters, telephone calls, delegations to City Hall, and letters to the press. After a public hearing filled with voices of protest from a large group from the South 72nd Street area, on January 6, 1961, the Common Council committee studying library matters finally decided to act. It voted to reverse the priorities for the southwest side libraries.

There was evidence enough to indicate that we were heading for a showdown in the council, and I wanted to make sure that my staff and I were ready. All along, my staff had been gathering various segments of research bearing on the library question, but more was needed for the decisive moment that would soon be facing me. Of even greater importance, it seemed to me, was the need for the development of a more formalized analysis of problems before a decision should be made.

Such a system of analysis had been one of my goals since I had taken office in April, but full development had been curtailed by the business of organization that faces any new administration. For some time now, however, I had tried to impress upon my staff the need for just such a systematic approach to decision making. Most of the staff had read Hodnett's *The Art of Problem Solving* and other sources dealing with this subject. The decision that faced us in the 72nd Street library situation was one that, more than any other problem of our new administration, called for a practical application of the scientific approach.

Our first attempt at such a formalized system came at this point as a memorandum from the staff member assigned to the matter. This analysis noted that some of the points made by the South 72nd Street groups had a certain amount of validity and that no equivalent interest had been expressed by citizens in the more easterly portions of the ward. It implied that a case could be made for approval of the South 72nd Street location, but also pointed to the undesirability of having priorities "presumably established by technically competent people after some study upset by neighborhood demands." Although the memorandum was a step forward in the process, I still did not feel that it covered sufficiently all of the factors that would enter into the final decision. I asked for further work, not only on research on the problem, but also toward development of a more schematic presentation of the factors.

Full action on the matter was delayed for two weeks through the efforts of those aldermen who were taking a city-wide view of this matter. During the delay, the first petition was received from persons favoring the South 35th Street site, but it was not enough to offset the outcry from opposing groups.

On January 24, 1961, the day the council finally met, I made another effort on behalf of a planned approach to city-wide library building and for preservation of the present priorities. I requested that the council return its files on the South 72nd Street library and library building priorities to the study committee. I asked that it determine, in cooperation with the Library Board, what principles should govern branch library location, size, priority, areas served, budgetary impact, types of services, and related matters. I also pointed out the need to integrate the library program into overall city capital improvement planning.

The council followed a portion of my recommendation and referred the question of future library locations—except for the South 72nd Street library—back to committee. By a vote of 15 to 5, it voted to go ahead with the construction of the westerly branch.

By this time, our formalized approach to decision making was beginning to reach the stage of the M-25. The analysis of the South 72nd Street library problems presented to me now consisted of research arranged under eleven general headings:

1. Statement of Problem Situation
2. Timetable
3. Basic Problem Statement
4. Facts Bearing on Problem
5. Assumptions
6. Critical Factors Affecting Decision
7. Alternatives Available
8. Recommendation
9. Other Ways of Stating Problem
10. Persons to Be Considered with Special Interest in Matter
11. Further Research Required

The recommendation based on the analysis was that the resolution favoring the 72nd Street location be vetoed. It went on to say, "The whole problem should be restudied and justification provided for each of the items on an approved priority schedule. Based on existing standards, a recommendation should be made that the site near South 35th Street be given top priority. This should serve to counteract most of the disappointment in this part of the city."

In my veto message, I said that the city should not build "the wrong type of building in the wrong place at the wrong time." I pointed out that the proposed site was too small to accommodate a building to meet generally accepted standards; that the more easterly location would serve a greater number of citizens; that the cost of operating two small libraries would be greater than that of operating one large facility; and that smaller libraries could not provide reading materials equal to those which could be made available at a single large regional branch. Finally, I noted that building on this site would result in a long-term deficit in the area's library resources, since relocation of the South 43rd Street library would then have to be placed at the bottom of the priority list.

Our calculations had been correct. The council failed to override the veto, and passed the resolution to purchase the site for a replacement of the South 43rd Street library. Ground for the new library was finally broken in June, 1962, thus vindicating my original judgment that construction funds would not be needed in the 1961 budget.

The city's biggest gain from the whole affair came in July, 1962, when the City Plan Commission, the Library Board, and the newly created Department of City Development submitted a joint ten-year program for library construction. Accepted by the Common Council, this program was the first in the city's history created with the complete formal cooperation of our planning agencies and librarians. It has served as a sound basis for action in this area. The city has made annual appropriations for branch library construction and the program is being implemented on schedule. The matter has now been largely removed from controversy, and the question of library location has been left at the technical level where it properly belongs. Policymakers need only determine the size of the construction program and the speed with which it can be carried out.

A gain to the Mayor's Office was development, at the staff level, of a formal method for dealing with decisions of this kind. The analysis presented to me prior to the veto decision became the basis for the formalized M-25, somewhat more elaborate and sophisticated than the original. In the 72nd Street library case, the systematized analysis we had been seeking for so long was not only evolved, but tested under fire and found fully operational.

The purpose in using the procedure of formal analysis of controversial problems, as typified by the M-25, is to ensure the inclusion of the greatest possible number of factors that have a bearing on the problem—both in the thinking of the staff in preparing its analysis and in the thinking of the mayor. It is true that not all of these factors may be relevant in every situation. It is also true that, even under a formal procedure, important factors that should be considered may be omitted or may not be considered properly. But a requirement for formal review of major factors bearing on a decision will reduce the possibility of omission or error. This possibility must be minimized both in staff analysis and in the mayor's own thinking. Of course, the final decision is the responsibility of the mayor. The primary purpose of the formal analysis, in brief, is to ensure that as many factors, viewpoints, and approaches as possible are pointed out in the course of the decision-making process.

As the library case points out, however, the overriding responsibility of the major is to apply a city-wide viewpoint based on the long-range interests of the community. To do this, he may have to disregard hurt feelings in particular areas. Aldermen elected on a district basis must always have one eye on their particular constituents. So must the mayor. The difference is that the mayor's constituency is the whole city. Only the mayor has the vantage point that enables him to carry out his obligation to take a city-wide view even on matters which sometimes appear to be purely parochial.

The Brown Deer Case

Some decisions are thrust upon the decision maker (as the previous case), some are matters of choice, and some are matters of heritage. The Brown Deer case falls into the last category. It is also a case in which the M-25 process came to full maturity (for an illustration of the use of the M-25 in this case, see the Appendix).

Geographically, what was involved in the Brown Deer case was an area of 16½ square miles located on the northwest edge of the City of Milwaukee, an area that had originally been a part of the former Town of Granville. In 1955, Milwaukee and Granville agreed to consolidate and the move was approved by referendums in both the city and the town in April, 1956.

An interested observer of the negotiations between the city and the town, and later an antagonist in the proceedings, was the Village of Brown Deer, which had previously incorporated out of the Town of Granville area. Before the voters of Milwaukee and Granville approved the referendums, representatives of Brown Deer moved into the act by adopting ordinances annexing to their own village 16½ square miles of the 22½ square miles that comprised Granville's total area. Following the referendums, Brown Deer challenged the consolidation, claiming that its annexation postings took precedence.

The issue moved into the courts, and in November,

1956, the State Supreme Court held that the territory of the former town was subject to annexation by the village, provided the outstanding annexation petitions were valid.

This decision threw the ball back to the City of Milwaukee which then challenged Brown Deer's annexation. The result was the longest circuit court trial in the history of Milwaukee County, ending in a decision which pleased neither the city nor the village. The court ruled that three of the petitions, affecting approximately 11 square miles, were faulty, and jurisdiction over this area passed to the City of Milwaukee. The other 5½ square miles, including some prime developmental land, remained in the jurisdiction of the Village of Brown Deer.

The court's decision actually hung on a slim thread. The court ruled that the Village of Brown Deer had failed to obtain the signatures of enough owners to represent more than a majority of the assessed value of the area. Out of a total valuation of many millions of dollars, only a few thousand dollars of assessed valuation made the difference. Hence, if a higher court decided in favor of the validity of only one or two of the signatures ruled invalid by the Circuit Court, the majority of the validation would swing in favor of Brown Deer.

Following the court's Solomon-like decision, it became apparent that neither party would be content with its allocated portion of the baby, and both Milwaukee and Brown Deer moved to take the case to the Supreme Court of the State of Wisconsin. However, both sides realized that a court test could be expensive and time-consuming and efforts were begun to negotiate a settlement.

This was the situation that confronted me soon after I took office, when I was approached by members of a negotiating committee to give my blessing to their efforts.

The importance of the case was not limited simply to the fact that if Milwaukee lost in the Supreme Court the city's expansion would be restricted. Of underlying significance was the fact that some of the disputed territory represented prime industrial land that would ensure the city's future economic growth.

My dilemma as mayor was multihorned. A cursory examination of the proposed settlement was enough to indicate to us that it was far from the most desirable settlement for the city. Yet, it was an agreement purportedly reached in good faith by representatives of the city and the village. Could I effectively renounce it and gain public support for the decision? Suppose that I turned it down and the Supreme Court decided to award the disputed area to Brown Deer? Wouldn't the city be better off with half a loaf, or even a few crumbs, than with nothing? In any event, I decided that any course of action would have to be based on facts and a rationale that could be intelligently defended.

To head off a hasty compromise, I took advantage of the requirements for agreement set down by state statutes pertaining to detachments and annexation. Under these, the settlement proposed by the negotiating committee required the approval of three-quarters of the members of the governing bodies of both Milwaukee and Brown Deer. At this stage of the game, however, it was possible for the Common Council to pass a resolution of intent by a simple majority rather than the three-fourths margin (15 council votes) that would be required for actual detachment ordinances. Appearing before the Common Council committee studying the proposed settlement, I made it clear that I would veto the resolution unless it could muster 15 affirmative votes in the council. I was fairly well convinced that a three-quarters vote was out of the question at the time and that this move would block quick efforts to push through the settlement.

Following this statement to the council, I assigned certain staff members to make a full M-25 analysis of the situation and present a staff recommendation. It was apparent from a preliminary study that if a valid decision was to be made, information was needed on the gross costs involved in bringing city improvements to the areas assigned to the city by the negotiators, together with a valid estimate of the revenues the city could expect from these areas. One of the tasks of the M-25 was to develop the statistical information on which a decision could be based.

Briefly, this entailed dissecting the land use plan for the area into quarter sections. Costs were then calculated for capital improvements and for services to each section. The ultimate population density, based on household units, was also projected. In addition, potential revenues from the area, after its full development, were calculated. The result was a breakdown for each square mile of taxable and non-taxable land usage, as well as a rough estimate of the net incremental value to the city of each of the 16½ square miles in the area involved. This provided a formidable tool for any discussion of settlement. For the first time, we had a complete picture of the figures we were dealing with whenever anyone talked about drawing suggested boundary lines on a map.

As negotiations continued, the economic analysis of the area was referred to time and time again. One of our principles of negotiation was that, as a minimum, the net incremental revenue for Milwaukee should be approximately 50 per cent of the value imputed to the total disputed area. With this in mind, my staff prepared at least thirty different proposed divisions of the disputed land, none of which satisfied both sides in the dispute.

In the meantime, I had proposed the hiring of outside legal counsel—an unprecedented step—to strengthen the city's hand in a court fight. Although the city has a very competent city attorney's office, the case to be argued before the Supreme Court revolved around many unprecedented legal questions. In making its decision, the circuit court had to rule on different aspects of corporate law, the law of estates, and many other legal points not related to municipal law. The alderman whose ward included the disputed area also believed that the city would be in a much better position if it employed outside counsel to present its case. There were some voices of dissent in the Common Council, but the proposal was finally accepted.

As the negotiations continued, the pressure mounted for settlement. Members of our official legal family, harried by the long battle and anxious about the outcome, were hesitant to predict the city's chances in a test before the Supreme Court. The head of the agency that had charge of the technical aspects of the matter seemed to be for settlement. He pointed out that we could also lose a new oil terminal which we had just wrested from a suburb and which had won us an important psychological victory. An alderman told me that he had "inside dope" from a Supreme Court justice that we would lose.

The well-qualified special counsel hired by the city gave me the guideline to the final course of action when he said, "A *good* settlement is better than a lawsuit." I knew, however, that a *good* settlement for Milwaukee would appear as an inferior settlement to Brown Deer. A fifty-fifty division based on our costs and potential revenues would be quite a different thing under its cost revenue structure. But the decision was now abundantly clear: I could offer nothing but a clear-cut fifty-fifty division, and this action would probably be tantamount to going to the Supreme Court. Such proved to be the case.

The majority of the Common Council seemed in a mood to accept a settlement that was inequitable according to the standards we had developed in my office. It was becoming obvious that if the case did go before the Supreme Court and we lost, the Common Council would hang the mayor in effigy from the top of our Flemish Renaissance City Hall tower.

Returning from official business in Washington, I found that the negotiating committee had taken matters into its own hands and settled for less than a fifty-fifty minimum division of potential revenues. The decision had been made by a majority of the committee. If our previous efforts were not to go down the drain, I knew that this settlement had to be stopped. There were other aspects of the settlement that bothered me. Who were some of the forces pushing for this settlement? Were certain developers and holders of land working behind the scenes?

As a first step, I publicly disavowed this proposed settlement, and did what I could to stall the proposal. Finally, after receiving a special letter from my office, the Judiciary Committee of the Common Council, acting as a standing committee, rejected the negotiating committee's proposal even though its members constituted a majority of that committee. Instead, the Judiciary Committee accepted a boundary adjustment along the lines of a division of potential revenues as I had proposed.

The decision was now made. This was our final offer—a division which our research showed to be equitable. The odds were that the offer would be spurned by Brown Deer officials and that action by the Supreme Court would follow. Amid much sound and fury, the offer was rejected by the Village Board. At this stage, I knew this was to be expected—but the decision had been made not to settle for anything less than a division that would be fair to the people of Milwaukee. If we could not have that, I had no qualms in facing the Supreme Court. It was better to go for broke than to bargain away the city's fair share of a common economic future.

In April, 1962, the Supreme Court handed down its decision. Our M-25 analysis was proved sound, and the steps we had taken to hire special counsel to strengthen our case paid off. The court decided that all of the annexations which Brown Deer claimed to have made, save one, were invalid, since some of the papers signed by heads of corporations had not been backed by official corporate action. The one exception was a golf course, which we were quite willing to concede to the village in return for land that could help ensure our city's industrial development.

NOTES

1. James Menzies Black, *How to Grow in Management* (Englewood Cliffs, N.J.: Prentice-Hall, Inc., 1957), pp. 85–95.

2. Edward Hodnett, *The Art of Problem Solving* (New York: Harper & Row, Publishers, 1955), pp. 1–4.

3. John Dewey, *How We Think* (Boston: D. C. Heath & Co., 1933).

4. John D. Millett, *Management in the Public Service* (New York: McGraw-Hill, Inc., 1954), p. 12.

5. Frederick D. Randall, "Stimulate Your Executives to Think Creatively," *Harvard Business Review,* XXXIII (July–August 1955) pp. 121–28.

6. Aurin Uris, *Developing Your Executive Skills* (New York: McGraw-Hill, 1955), pp. 50–58.

7. Robert Lovett, one-time Secretary of Defense, used the phrase in an appearance before a congressional subcommittee to describe the device of inviting argument between conflicting interests.

8. Hodnett, *op. cit.*

eight *A Philosophy of Local Leadership*

As we reach the final P of the D-STEPP formula, these questions remain: What operating perspective may be distilled from the previous discussions and cases cited? What should be the mayor's basic approach to the establishment of goals and policy, the communication of a common purpose, the influencing of people? What philosophy or system can we evolve for guiding the public life of the top municipal executive?

In laying down a set of tentative answers to these questions, we almost automatically rotate backward through the formula to begin again with an elaboration of the very definition of institutional leadership given in the introduction.

Further Definition of Institutional Leadership

A responsible institutional leader avoids both utopianism and opportunism. To avoid opportunism, he shuns the short-run advantage, or the quick disposition, in favor of the long-run benefit to the institution.[1]

For instance, he does not piously proclaim that there "should be better planning" and orderly programming of such matters as library priorities and then yield to a pressure group that will sabotage the whole premise of proper programming. He does not, opportunistically, gain the favor of the pressure group to the long-run disadvantage of his city (this was the issue in the 72nd Street library case). He does not accept a safe, quick disposition (as in the Brown Deer case), when the greater advantage to his city lies overwhelmingly in an alternative. Above all, he does not let the institutional character of his city suffer from a movement of his government based on sheer drift rationalized into a policy.

As he strives to exercise the creative aspects of institutional leadership, he must try to read the hopes of his city. He must try to relate these hopes to his programming; this is the basis of his strategy. Conversely, in his effort to communicate, he relates his programming to those happenings that affect the lives of people in their direct hopes, expectations, and frustrations; this is part of his effort toward enrollment.

He therefore develops a strategy related to the things people want and need. They have to make a living, to pay the grocery bill and the rent or mortgage payments. They want their city and its neighborhood kept in good condition—clean, bright, and attractive. If they are old, they want appreciation, companionship, and possibly help. If they are young, they want appreciation and opportunity. If they are members of the solid middle class—workingmen, tradesmen, or white collar employees—or if they are businessmen, professional men, or industrialists, they want a decent community where services are good. Whatever their station in life, they want a good educational and recreational climate for their children.

Their hopes in a big city embrace more than orthodox municipal service; they embrace the physical, the economic, and the social environment of the community. And these expectations have added new burdens to the office of mayor. The day of the simple municipal service government is gone. A new era has arrived, in which the big test of a mayor is whether he can cope with the demands and needs for economic, social, and physical development.

As he proceeds, he must have a most subtle understanding of his role in working to fill the needs of the people. He knows that he can never hope for perfect solutions to his city's problems—only satisfactory ones. He recognizes further that, in the overpowering tasks of his position, something will always go amiss. And because of the limitations on his position (limitations of time, of resources, of authority) some things must of necessity be neglected. But he can show the people that he is fighting for their needs. And the more they are convinced that he is trying to suit their wishes and needs, the more they tend to excuse or rationalize (or even misinterpret in his favor) his actions when he takes an opposing point of view.

Furthermore, there is one need that he can often fulfill—the need for recognition. (It seems an established condition of human behavior that people seek virtue through reason far less than they seek approval from the people around them and that generally man seeks community

approval more than political power or economic riches).[2]
Although the chief executive often can do little to change
hard reality, he can bestow much nonmaterial gratification,
which is more important to many people. By language,
spoken or written, he can show respect, and thereby give
honor or status.

Involvement with Strategy

The mayor should think of leadership as a function. He
must specialize in obtaining information, conveying ideas,
and policing an information-processing system that solves
problems. His main personal objective as a leader is to
build a problem-solving organization. In this organization,
he must encourage people to carry out specialized roles.
Whatever his choices or decisions may be, he moves in a
world of strategy and tactics deeply involved with gaining
the consent of others.[3]

In a free city like Milwaukee, he must bear in mind at all
times a fundamental of human behavior—that his citizens
and the people with whom he deals are less concerned with
their personal exercise of power than they are with the
possibility that he may become too powerful, and they will
always seek ways to limit his power. Therefore, the rule
holds most forcefully for him that he must induce people
to participate in his plans before he moves. He can almost
never prevail simply by his own will in the freest of cities
with its polylithic power structure; he must move with at
least a squadron if he is to win an encounter. This is a basic
lesson of the case histories I have given here.

Involvement with Tactics: Relationship with Groups

As the cases generally illustrate, a leader would do well to keep in mind and learn all he can about the conduct of groups, for the reservoir of his tactical strength consists in his understanding of the performance of groups.

In dealing with the Common Council, for example, one must remember that the group strongly influences the behavior of the members because the group supports or reinforces the cooperative members of the group or punishes members who rebel against its norms. So, in his approach to the council, he must seek to avoid antagonizing the council in such a way that attitudes will be conditioned permanently against him. He never attacks the council as a body; he seldom replies to attacks from its individual members. Further, he must seek ways to show his respect for the habits and persons of the group without lowering his own standards.

Whenever he strikes an issue, such as a pay raise for his staff, on which he can develop little outside assistance, the mayor is up against absolute control by the council, and he had better realize this. The group decides for itself what is correct, and there is unlikely to be any sort of significant external help for his position. On such an issue, he cannot even fight an effective public battle; few will support a pay raise for his people, no matter how good his case. Here he must often wait until a majority can be persuaded to support his request, or until other issues that may have created a situation which found frustrations expressed in complete opposition to his proposal have been resolved.

He must find ways, personally or through third parties, to ascertain the interaction among the members of the council, to judge the opinion of the council in order to have a reliable guide for his own behavior. Since there is constant interaction, this is a constant task.

There is a key to individual behavior in conjunction with groups that no local leader should ever forget: In maintaining man's morale, *the small group around the subject is often more important than the large issues involved in political affairs.* The individual votes with his friends as well as for the candidate. Often what is right is what one's peers agree is right.[4] The greatest single authority over the life of the individual would seem to be the authority of the group. (When an individual feels uncomfortable with this authority, he leaves the group.) *In testing sentiment of a formal group such as the Common Council, the mayor had best know the sentiment of the subgroups or informal groups.* For, as this sentiment jells, so will his program jell as they act upon it.

He must also recognize certain fundamentals about operating as the leader of a group. These are:

1. *He knows that the product of discussion by a group (five to seven for informality) is better than with individuals.* In a group, people are stimulated to produce, and many facets of an issue are revealed from different points of view. He recognizes that groups are likely to function best when the responsibility for action involves the entire group. He also knows that he had better fix responsibility for coordinated action on an individual after the group meets.

2. *If he genuinely wants participation by the group, he had better keep his planning general and without predeter-*

mined conclusions. Otherwise, his participants will anticipate the conclusions and tend to either resist, rubber-
stamp, or withdraw without feeling that they are really
participants.

3. *He must clarify objectives so that everyone knows
where the project is headed and anyone can withdraw if he
chooses.* He should poll the group, and as the group pro-
gresses, he should be alert for subtle goal displacement.

4. *He should realize that every meeting has a hidden
agenda which consists of the motivations of the members,
power, prestige, etc.* He should therefore look for opportunities to advance the personal goals of members, where
these are compatible with group goals, to increase the
effectiveness of the group.

5. *Occasionally, he ought to poll the group on how the
members feel about the group's progress.* The group should
be furnished the opportunity to relieve frustration so that
change can come about (and change gets better support if
it is discussed with the group rather than with individual
members) and valid communication be maintained.

6. *Decisions should come only after everybody has had a
chance to speak his peace; otherwise, vague feelings of
hostility and eventual sabotage may follow.* Research shows
that decisions are most likely to be carried into action if
they are group-consensus decisions, when the members by
their own efforts can settle on a choice. Decisions imposed
by a majority or by a leader are not likely to be effective. If
total agreement cannot be reached, there must at least be
agreement that action is needed. The minority may be
more amenable after it has had a chance to express itself.

As Ordway Tead has put it: "There can be little ques-

tion that partial consent is better than no consent or en-
forced consent, due to the absence of any prior sharing in
discussion and decision. Also partial consent after delibera-
tion is one of the ways toward eventually more complete
agreement."[5]

Enrollment: The People a Mayor Depends On

The mayor should seek to enroll his institution in a high
purpose. Such an effort has been made in the attempt to
enroll Milwaukee in strategic and tactical planning; that is,
analyzing the environment to determine how best to use
the existing resources and capabilities through such means
as the Community Renewal Program and the social development and economic development programs. Our
effort is called the "Milwaukee Idea," a name that exempli-
fies a unified sense of mission. This is reinforced by a conception of leadership that has been most aptly expressed by
the Municipal Manpower Commission in its report, *Governmental Manpower for Tomorrow's Cities*. In speaking
of the public executive, the report states, "What distin-
guishes him most is his ability to achieve consensus at the
highest possible level with the greatest benefit to the entire
community and then to follow through with action. . . ."[6]

In order to do this, he must strain to the utmost to keep
his program before those whose loyalty he would command, sharing the limelight with them, building their sense
of participation, showing as clearly as possible that the
project is more important than personal considerations. At
the same time, he must realize that those he depends on

have other loyalties that may override loyalty to his projects and that he must be willing to help them—perhaps do favors for them—to strengthen his position in competing with the other loyalties.[7] (At times, if he is sure that it will please them, he can ask them to do a particular thing for him that he knows they do well and enjoy doing.) He knows that his most effective pattern of leadership is evidenced by setting objectives and that at times he must make challenging demands to stimulate interest. He avoids close checking, however. In addition, although he should be a "person" (not detached or aloof), some social distance and independence from subordinates will probably make him more effective.[8]

He ought to get to know as much as he can about the people he depends on. Their factual history is not as important as their dominant likes and fears—the way they *feel* about things. This will enable him to estimate the meaningfulness of his potential actions to them.[9] If he wishes to change an individual he depends upon, he must use extreme caution in giving advice; it may violate the other person's defenses or be misunderstood and put into operation poorly, and he will be blamed.[10] If he wants a change, he must concentrate on helping the other fellow change himself. The other fellow must assume responsibility for the change, because of his superior knowledge of his situation. The mayor is just the helper.

Because he is surrounded by human reactions, by the reactions of individuals, groups, institutional leaders, the mass public, the most significant part of his philosophy of leadership must be his understanding of and approach to people. Basically, he might be guided by certain tested assumptions about people: that their feeling of insecurity must never be underestimated, that as a consequence of it they cling to old habits, familiar methods, and immediate security. In this knowledge, he must act to effect change only after involving the people who must effect the change.

People do not change (to act on anything new or to take initiative or to give up a prejudice) unless there is a stimulus or until they feel uncomfortable. The mayor can contribute to this feeling by raising the level of aspiration so that the changee finds his old behavior inadequate and awkward. Another way is to enlist a third party to use his effectiveness to make the changee uncomfortable. (The "third party" as I mean it here may be references, statistics, and authority—presentations through written matter that stimulate thinking.)

Involvement with Power

The mayor learns that his formal authority may give him status, but that its most effective use is limited to situations calling for immediate action. He learns that command is not as effective a tool as is skill in human relations or mutual understanding. (However, his status sometimes bars him from such understanding, for some will tell him what they think he wants to hear and others will tell him things to alarm him in order to manipulate him.) He learns that even with his immediate staff his formal authority will "promote compliance with directives and discipline, but does not encourage employees to exert effort, to accept responsibilities, or to exercise initiative."[11] He faces the problems of all supervisors in finding ways to extend his influence beyond the narrow limits of formal authority.

To be sure, the leader cannot ignore the environment. His job is to test the environment to find out which pressures and demands can truly threaten him, to change the environment by finding allies and sources of external support, and to gird his organization by creating the means and the will to withstand attacks.[12] He had better know that he lives with a continuous degree of hostility and sometimes the cruelty of uncompromising opposition, with continuous threats to his authority as well as multiple demands upon his energy and his time.

There is a time for a mayor to fight and a time not to fight. He should not waste his ammunition on petty opposition or carping criticism about minor injustice. A responsible mayor should never dissipate his energy on matters that are not productive of progress. He *should* fight on important projects or programs and to combat serious attacks on his public prestige. He fights by attempting to win the cooperation of the necessary allies and by selecting his targets for opposition with great care (a carefully selected enemy can do his cause much good). And when he attacks he must "take the enemy at his weakest," as the proverb says.

But there are also other proverbs he should keep in mind. He must remember that on a particular issue argument seldom convinces anyone against his inclination and that during the battle and afterwards good language often cures great sores. More than anyone else in his city, the mayor should remember that man's evil comes from frustration, not from inherent nature—that this is often the basis of his opposition and that certainly it is the basis of antisocial action.

Conclusion

It would be relatively easy for the mayor to concentrate simply on the brush fires, on the issues of the day that are relevant to visible situations. Although he cannot ignore these, he must carry water on both shoulders if he is to be a responsible institutional leader.

The central city mayor survives only when he has the psychological capacity and the resourcefulness to handle at one time three man-eating gorillas of crises and two of the paper tigers that, it seems at times, are thrown upon his back just to test him. He must be Leavitt's "rare third man," who, in his reaction to frustration, "starts thinking about where to go from there . . . very few incidents in his lifetime would include insurmountable obstacles (because he would always have ways around them) . . . his self-esteem would be so solid that few things could threaten it. His egotistic needs instead would be needs for accomplishment of organizational goals."[13]

Whatever a mayor's choices or decisions may be, the desired results of his public leadership can be vetoed by others—by the Common Council (or its equivalent in his city), by department heads, by the channels of communication, or by the combined opposition of groups—unless he has carefully reckoned with the human element. For him the maxim most strongly applies, "For the burden and the benefit come from the same source; life, and reality, is other people."[14]

NOTES

1. Philip Selznick, *Leadership in Public Administration* (New York: Harper & Row, Publishers, 1957).

2. Bernard Berelson and Gary A. Steiner, *Human Behavior* (New York: Harcourt, Brace and World, 1964), p. 666.

3. Harold J. Leavitt, *Managerial Psychology* (Chicago: The University of Chicago Press, 1958), p. 229.

4. Berelson and Steiner, *op. cit.*, p. 335.

5. Ordway Tead, *Management in the Public Service* (New York: McGraw-Hill, Inc., 1951).

6. Municipal Manpower Commission, *Governmental Manpower for Tomorrow's Cities* (New York: McGraw-Hill, Inc., 1962), p. 22.

7. Peter M. Blau and W. Richard Scott, *Formal Organizations* (San Francisco: Chandler Publishing Co., 1962), p. 142.

8. *Ibid.*, p. 153.

9. Leavitt, *op. cit.*, p. 165.

10. *Ibid.*, p. 164.

11. Blau and Scott, *op. cit.*, p. 140.

12. Selznick, op. cit.

13. Leavitt, *op. cit.*, p. 44.

14. Berelson and Steiner, *op. cit.*, p. 665.

bibliography

Books

Edward C. Banfield and James Q. Wilson, *City Politics* (Cambridge, Mass.: Harvard University Press and the M.I.T. Press, 1963).

Bernard Berelson and Gary A. Steiner, *Human Behavior* (New York: Harcourt, Brace and World, 1964).

James Menzies Black, *How to Grow in Management* (Englewood Cliffs, N.J.: Prentice-Hall, Inc., 1957).

Peter M. Blau and W. Richard Scott, *Formal Organizations* (San Francisco: Chandler Publishing Co., 1962).

Daniel W. Hoan, *City Government* (New York: Harcourt, Brace and Company, 1936).

Edward Hodnett, *The Art of Problem Solving* (New York: Harper & Row, Publishers, 1955).

Harold J. Leavitt, *Managerial Psychology* (Chicago: The University of Chicago Press, 1958).

John D. Millett, *Management in the Public Service* (New York: McGraw-Hill, Inc., 1954).

Municipal Manpower Commission, *Governmental Manpower for Tomorrow's Cities* (New York: McGraw-Hill, Inc., 1962).

Richard E. Neustadt, *Presidential Power* (New York: John Wiley & Sons, 1960).

Harvey S. Perloff, *Planning and the Urban Community* (Pittsburgh: University of Pittsburgh Press, 1961).

Wallace S. Sayre and Herbert Kaufman, *Governing New York City* (New York: Russell Sage Foundation, 1960).

Philip Selznick, *Leadership in Public Administration* (New York: Harper & Row, Publishers, 1957).

Bayard Still, *Milwaukee* (Madison: The State Historical Society of Wisconsin, 1948).

Ordway Tead, *Management in the Public Service* (New York: McGraw-Hill, Inc., 1951).

Aurin Uris, *Developing Your Executive Skills* (New York: McGraw-Hill, Inc., 1955).

Articles and Reports

Advisory Commission on Intergovernmental Relations, *Metropolitan Social and Economic Disparities: Implications for Intergovernmental Relations in Central Cities and Suburbs* (Washington, D.C.: U.S. Government Printing Office, 1965).

American Society of Planning Officials, *The Community Renewal Program: The First Years*, a report prepared by Jerome L. Kaufman, Principal Planner, American Society of Planning Officials (Chicago: American Society of Planning Officials, 1963).

Seymour Freedgood, "New Strength in City Hall," in *The Exploding Metropolis* (Garden City, N.Y.: Doubleday Anchor Books, 1958).

Luther Gulick, "Notes on the Theory of Organization," in Luther Gulick and L. Urwick (eds.), *Papers on the Science of Administration* (New York: Columbia University Institute of Public Administration, 1937).

C. E. Lindblom, "The Science of Muddling Through," *Public Administration Review*, XIX (Spring 1959).

Norton E. Long, "The Local Community as an Ecology of Games," in Oliver P. Williams and Charles Press (eds.), *Democracy in Urban America* (Chicago: Rand McNally & Co., 1961).

appendix

STAFF REPORT   OFFICE OF THE MAYOR
CITY OF MILWAUKEE

(Note: Where space is insufficient attach an appendix)

I. PRELIMINARY ANALYSIS

A. Problem Identification:

   *Should Milwaukee accept
proposed settlement in five
disputed areas in the former
Town of Granville?*

Date of report _____

Common Council file # _____

Analyst _____

Target date for action _____

Originator _____

B. Description: Problem Situation and Its History (Outline):

*Milwaukee and Granville voted to consolidate in 1956. Several annexa-
tions to Brown Deer were pending at the time. These areas totaling 16
square miles have been under litigation since 1956. Latest decision
(May 1959) by Circuit Court declared Corrigan, Laun and Brown
Deer Park annexations invalid and Johnson and Tripoli annexations
valid, giving 11.36 square miles to Milwaukee and 5.00 square miles
to Brown Deer.*

*Decisions have been appealed and are now being considered by the
Supreme Court. Negotiating committee has proposed a settlement that
would among other things, give Milwaukee 7.00 square miles and
Brown Deer 9.36 square miles.*

C. Scope of Analysis (Financial, Legal, Organizational, Administrative
Questions):

*This analysis seeks to answer the question of whether Milwaukee
should accept the settlement proposed by the negotiating committee*

by evaluating the advantages and disadvantages along with the legal, financial, political and other implications of the settlement.

D. Facts Assembled (Financial, Legal Organizational, Administrative, etc.; give source):	Relative Weights		
	1*	2*	3*

Facts bearing on the question of whether Milwaukee should attempt to negotiate a settlement:

1. General facts

a. Milwaukee has a moral obligation to live up to the 1956 consolidation agreement with the residents in the former Town of Granville. It should be noted, however, that property owners holding 49.74% of the property valuation voted for annexation to Brown Deer and that others bought land after the consolidation vote.

Current ownership records show that around 60 parcels of land or 5 acres or more totaling 2,300 acres are under different ownership now than they were at the time of the consolidation.   **X**

b. Milwaukee won the Circuit Court decision on the Corrigan area. Its position is supported by a learned trial judge, who arrived at a decision after evaluating all of the facts in the case.   **X**

c. Milwaukee's margin of victory on the 10.5 sq. mi. Corrigan Area was very narrow. Brown Deer's annexation of this area was declared invalid because property owners signing annexation petitions did not account for 50% or more of the total assessed valuation, as required by statute. The actual figures reported in the court proceedings are as follows: **X**

Total assessed valuation (A.V.)	Amount $3,863,796.53	% of Total 100.00
A. V. property owners signing petition	$1,922,775.25	49.76

From these figures it can be determined that the city's margin of victory was $9,123.01, or 0.24 per cent of the total assessed valuation.

d. A reversal by the Supreme Court of one or more decisions allotting an additional $9,123.01 in assessed valuation to the petitioners favoring annexation would reverse the case and Milwaukee would lose the entire 10.5 square miles.   **X**

* 1. Very great importance. 2. Important. 3. Least important.

e. There is no way of predicting what the Supreme Court decision will be. Even our attorneys are not able to assess the City's chances of winning the case.   X

f. Some city and village officials and property owners in disputed areas are anxious to settle out of court to eliminate uncertainty and avoid further legal costs. (To date Brown Deer has spent $50,000–$75,000 on litigation.)   X

2. Legal facts

a. Legal difficulties anticipated under present law will be eliminated by Bill No. 39A now awaiting the signature of the Governor.   X

b. Bill No. 39A will also simplify procedure for settling by permitting approval of boundary settlement by simple majority of Common Council instead of three-quarter majority and approval of a majority of owners of three-fourths of property now required in areas to be detached.   X

3. Financial facts

a. The cost of public improvements chargeable to the city budget would vary with the type of development and the extent to which development would take place under the new platting law requiring installation of improvements by developers. The net cost in residential areas would vary from $4,155,000 to $6,067,000 per sq. mi. and would total $1,668,000 per sq. mi. in industrial areas.   X

b. The net budgetary impact of different types of development is difficult to determine due to problems in estimating revenues and operating costs. (Staff has estimated a net surplus of $100,000–$150,000 per sq. mi. for a hypothetical residential area.)   X

Additional facts bearing on the question of whether Milwaukee should accept the proposed settlement:

1. Division of the 16.36 sq. mi. under dispute in the proposed settlement is as follows:

	Area (sq. mi.)	Percent
Milwaukee	7.00	42.0
Brown Deer	9.36	57.5
Total	16.36	100.0

Other boundary adjustments would give 80 arces of city land to Brown Deer.		X
2. Of the total assessed valuation of nearly $16.0 million, 81% ($13 million) would go to Brown Deer and 19% ($3 million) to Milwaukee.		X
3. Milwaukee would give Brown Deer 5.24 sq. mi. of land assessed at $4,589,800, while Brown Deer would give Milwaukee 0.75 sq. mi. assessed at $403,670.	X	
4. 57% of the developable area in the Corrigan area would stay in Milwaukee and 43% would go to Brown Deer. Industrial land would be divided equally and residential land 60–40 with 60% to Milwaukee.	X	
5. 71% of the land in the Corrigan area going to Milwaukee would be residential, 1% commercial and 28% industrial. Land going to Brown Deer would be 63% residential, 1% commercial, and 36% industrial.	X	
6. Three-fourths of Milwaukee's industrial land would be located in the extreme northwestern part of the county. To serve this area, city facilities will have to be extended a distance of 3 to 4 miles, 1 to 2 miles of which would be in Brown Deer.	X	
7. All of the area that would go to Milwaukee is relatively isolated and intruded with large public areas which would add to the cost of municipal improvements.		X

E. Assumptions:

1. Milwaukee has an interest in acquiring additional land in the former Town of Granville.

2. Milwaukee could use land for industry to build the employment base and tax base and for high quality residential development to build leadership potential and help strengthen tax base. We should avoid annexing vast areas to be used for housing in the lower and middle price ranges. This view is based on the assumption that this type of residential development is a financial liability to the city because of the relatively high demand for city services and facilities and the relatively low tax yields. Studies supporting this view have been challenged on the grounds that:

a. They are based on unrealistic assignment of benefits from municipal services and facilities and the costs thereof.

b. They ignore the principle of ability to pay in taxation.

Staff has completed cost-revenue studies which indicate that residential areas yield sufficient revenues to offset operating costs and to amortize capital expenditures over a relatively short period and yield a profit. ($100,000–$150,000 per sq. mi.) Other arguments against this approach can be found in statements made during the past decade in support of Milwaukee's aggressive expansion policies.

Another implied assumption is that the powerful trend toward decentralization can be checked or reversed through an active urban renewal program. This may prove to be a false assumption if we continue to subsidize suburban-type living through the many tax and other programs of federal, state and local governments and fail to channel adequate resources into rebuilding older areas of the city.

If we can't attract people and business firms to the central city, we had better annex any areas that we can to offset the decline in population, tax base and employment base that is bound to continue in these areas.

3. Milwaukee has the best chance of winning the Supreme Court case and therefore should negotiate from a position of strength.

4. Bill No. 39A will be signed by the Governor, thus clearing all legal obstacles to a settlement.

5. Milwaukee has a moral obligation to the people who voted for consolidation. It is assumed that people who signed the annexation petition to Brown Deer voted against consolidation. Milwaukee has no obligation to these people or to those who bought property in the area after the consolidation vote.

6. It is assumed that the city can and will exercise more effective control over the type and rate of development in new areas and can effectively resist the strong pressures that are likly to develop to weaken these controls as time goes on regardless of how much land we get in the disputed areas.

7. Brown Deer will accept a settlement that is more favorable to Milwaukee if the city holds firm to its position.

F. Alternative Solutions and Consequences:

Solution #1—Accept settlement proposed by negotiating committee

Advantages

1. The proposed settlement appears to be acceptable to the Brown Deer Village Board.

2. It gives Milwaukee 840 acres of land for industry and large areas suitable for high-quality residential development.

3. We avoid the risk of losing the whole Corrigan area in an adverse Supreme Court decision.

4. It would assure that the pipeline terminal would be in the city.

5. It would eliminate the uncertainty and further legal costs.

Disadvantages

1. We fail to meet our moral obligations to the many people who voted for consolidation and who would be in the areas going to Brown Deer.

2. Terms do not accurately reflect the fact that Milwaukee has a better chance of winning the Corrigan area than Brown Deer.

3. Terms are weighted too heavily in favor of Brown Deer on the division of land area, tax base and development potential.

4. Brown Deer gets the choice industrial land.

5. Net average capital cost per square mile for public improvements in the Corrigan area charged to the general city budget would be $120,000–$150,000 higher for Milwaukee than they would be if we get the whole area.

7. Aggrieved property owners might initiate court action challenging the settlement and start a new round of litigation.

Solution #2—Reject present settlement and let matter go through court.

Advantages

1. City meets its moral obligation to people who voted for consolidation.

2. We eliminate the risk of any future court action from property owners aggrieved by a settlement out of court.

4. If we win we get all 10.5 sq. mi. of land in the Corrigan area including 1,700 acres of good industrial land.

5. Because of the higher percentage of industrial land, the net average capital cost per square mile of providing public improvements in the Corrigan area would be $120,000–$150,000 less than it would be for the 6.25 sq. mi. going to the city under the proposed settlement.

Disadvantages

1. We run the risk of losing the Supreme Court decision and the whole 10.5 sq. mi. in the Corrigan area.

2. We may be criticized for being uncooperative and for prolonging the litigation and the uncertainty in the area.

3. If we win we assume the financial burden of developing 10.5 sq. mi. of open land. Budgetary impact can be controlled by regulating the type and rate of development but in practice this is a very difficult task.

4. If we lose we will be criticized for not negotiating for part of the area when we had the chance.

5. If we lose we get none of the 10.5 sq. mi. and we lose around 1,700 acres of good industrial land and the last opportunity to get sizable land areas suitable for high-income housing.

6. If we lose Brown Deer might start making tax deals with industry and become our most important competitor for industrial development.

Solution # 3—Reject present settlement and propose alternative settlement discussed under Item II-D below.

Advantages

1. We avoid risk of losing the whole Corrigan area.

2. We eliminate uncertainty in the disputed areas and avoid further legal costs.

3. It would assure that pipeline terminal would be in the city.

4. Terms of the alternative settlement more accurately reflect the relative strength of Milwaukee and Brown Deer in the Supreme Court case.

5. Under the alternative settlement Milwaukee would get 620 acres more industrial land than under the present settlement.

6. In general the terms of the alternative settlement are more advantageous to Milwaukee with respect to the division of land, tax base and development potential.

7. The net average capital cost of public improvements per square mile under the alternative settlement would be $60,000–$75,000 less than if we develop the whole 10.5 sq. mi. and $180,000–$230,000 less than if we develop the 6.25 sq. mi. under the proposed settlement.

8. The alternative settlement requires that school district boundaries be settled before any municipal boundaries become effective.

9. Since we would get more land we would be living up to our moral obligation with more people than would be the case under the present settlement.

Disadvantages

1. The alternative settlement might not be acceptable to Brown Deer.

2. We do not meet our moral obligation to all people who voted for consolidation.

3. We run the risk of possible future court action by aggrieved property owners, although the risk is smaller than it would be if we accept the negotiating committee settlement.

Solution #4—Lose the Supreme Court case deliberately and show no further interest in the five disputed areas.

Advantages

1. We avoid all financial problems and other difficulties resulting from developing new areas.

2. We can concentrate all energy and resources on preserving and rebuilding older sections of city. (See comment under E-2 above)

3. We eliminate the uncertainty in the area and avoid further legal costs.

Disadvantages

1. We ignore completely our obligations to the people who voted for consolidation.

2. We break faith with oil companies involved in oil terminal project.

3. We will lose tax base from oil terminal and opportunity to get large tracts of good industrial land.

4. Brown Deer would get a large supply of industrial land and might become an important competitor for industrial development.

5. We lose opportunity to expand in area and maintain city's relative political power at the state and county levels, and minimize the problems of fragmented government.

6. We lose opportunity to acquire large tracts of land suitable for high-quality residential development.

7. We abandon opportunity to acquire a large area, which if properly developed, could become a real asset to the city, financially and otherwise.

8. We are staking the city's future entirely on the success of one program; namely, urban renewal. (See comment under E-2 above)

9. We lose other advantages which Milwaukee officials have claimed from an aggressive annexation policy.

II. EVALUATION   F.A.R.

A. Public Relations (Group or Individuals Affected):	Alternative #				Relative Weights*
	1	2	3	4	
Residents in disputed areas	+	−	+	+	2
Developers in disputed areas	−	+	+	−	3
Oil companies who will build oil terminal	+	−	+	−	
Builders and related groups	−	+	+	−	3
Labor unions, especially building trades	−	+	+	−	3
General public	?	?	?	?	1
Residents of Brown Deer	+	?	?	+	4
Suburban residents	+	−	?	+	4
B. Official Relations (Groups or Individuals Affected):					
Aldermen generally	−	+	+	−	1
Aldermen in favor of settlement	+	−	−	−	2
Brown Deer Village officials	+	−	?	+	4
Suburban officials generally	+	−	−	+	4
C. Press:					
Reaction to ideas of a settlement has been favorable. One writer has said that Milwaukee is getting short end of deal in proposed settlement.)	+	−	+	?	

* 1. Very great importance. 2. Very important. 3. Important. 4. Least important.

D. Recommendation:

1. Call City Attorney in to discuss informally with the Mayor the city's chances of winning the case. Reject the proposed settlement because it is weighted too heavily in favor of Brown Deer.

2. Continue to negotiate not because our position is weak but to bargain away the areas that are likely to be expensive to develop.

3. Insist on a settlement that is more favorable to Milwaukee and that permits us to live up to our moral obligation to the people who voted for consolidation.

4. The following settlement terms are recommended:

a. All litigation is to be terminated and all appeals dismissed. (This action will not be necessary if Bill 39A is approved. The bill has passed the Legislature and is now awaiting the signature of the Governor.)

b. Disputed areas are to be divided, it being understood that every effort will be made to retain in Milwaukee property owners who resided in the Corrigan area at the time of the original consolidation and who did not sign the petition for annexation to Brown Deer.

c. Brown Deer agrees to reimburse Milwaukee for $74,000 in non-assessable funds spent on water mains in the Laun area.

d. Both parties agree to waive any claims under Section 66.03 of the Wisconsin Statutes relating to the adjustment of assets and liabilities.

e. Both parties agree that accrued highway aids shall be distributed on the basis of the boundaries specified in #2 above.

f. These conditions are to become effective only after all issues relating to joint school districts 3 and 4 are resolved to the satisfaction of the Common Council and the Village Board.

The following areas and factors should be held for further bargaining by the city:

(a) Two square miles of land bounded by North 76th Street, Brown Deer Road, North 107th Street and North County Line Road.

(b) One quarter square mile of land bounded by North 76th Street, Calumet Road, North 84th Street extended and Bradley Road.

(c) Approximately 80 acres of land in City of Milwaukee near Babolink and North 119th Street.

(d) Remove requirement for reimbursing Milwaukee for water main expenditures of $74,000 in Laun area. The advantages and disadvantages of this alternative settlement have already been listed under item f above.

5. Formulate a development program and policy for the area regardless of whether or not we negotiate a settlement.

E. Action Advised:

1. Get staff agreement on settlement terms and strategy.

2. Brief aldermen thoroughly on all aspects of matter.

3. Brief press and other groups to gain outside support.

4. Get agreement among aldermen on settlement terms and present to Brown Deer.

5. Get agreement among aldermen on development policy and program for the area. This should be done whether or not we negotiate a settlement.

index